The Noise

Now what has fallen where,
oh my
world?

Henry Braun

Also by Naomi Shihab Nye

POETRY
Fuel
Red Suitcase
Words Under the Words

ESSAYS
Never in a Hurry

PARAGRAPHS
Mint
Mint Snowball

NOVEL
Habibi

ANTHOLOGIES
The Space Between Our Footsteps:
Poems and Paintings from the Middle East

I Feel a Little Jumpy Around You:
*A Book of Her Poems &
His Poems Collected in Pairs
(with Paul B. Janeczko)*

The Tree Is Older Than You Are:
*A Bilingual Gathering of Poems and Stories
from Mexico*

This Same Sky:
A Collection of Poems from Around the World

Salting the Ocean

PICTURE BOOKS
Lullaby Raft
Benito's Dream Bottle
Sitti's Secrets
Come with Me:
Poems for a Journey

What have you lost?

Poems selected by

Naomi Shihab Nye

A GREENWILLOW BOOK

Harper
tempest

An Imprint of HarperCollins*Publishers*

In memory of

Beryl Baird
Maggie Cousins
Jim Talbot
David Bowen
Jim Tilton
Camille Domangue
Jaime Murphy
D'Ann Johnson
Bill Rips
Julia Cauthorn
John J. Santos, Jr.

Treasured friends of San Antonio,
you will never be lost to our hearts.

What Have You Lost?
Copyright © 1999 by Naomi Shihab Nye

Pages 192–200 constitute an extension of the copyright page.

Library of Congress Cataloging-in-Publication Data
Nye, Naomi Shihab.
What have you lost? / poems selected by Naomi Shihab Nye.
p.   cm.
"Greenwillow Books."
Summary: A collection of poems that explore all kinds of loss.
ISBN 0-688-16184-7 — ISBN 0-380-73307-2 (pbk.)
1. Loss (Psychology)—Poetry. 2. Young adult poetry. [1. Poetry—Collections.]
I. Nye, Naomi Shihab.
PN6109.97.W47 1999   98-26674
808.81'9353—dc21   CIP
                                                                              AC

First Harper Tempest edition, 2001
❖
Visit us on the World Wide Web!
www.harperteen.com

Contents

Introduction

I left my beloved gray linen neck pillow scented with lavender on an airplane yesterday. We had been on so many trips together. I didn't think of it until I was on another airplane. Stunned by my carelessness, I closed my eyes and could conjure perfectly its familiar nubby shape, but still had to wait till we landed to file a lost pillow report. I didn't have much faith I'd see it again. I've never gotten anything back from an airplane.

At ten, I treasured a burgundy velvet pouch filled with lost teeth. I carried it around with me, though no one else seemed interested in my macabre collection. One day, as my family rode a steamboat back and forth on the Mississippi River, I dropped the pouch overboard and sobbed. My father said, "Now the river will keep it for you!" This was not comforting at all.

By the time I was fifteen, things were worse, swirling with complications. I went to three different high schools and seemed to gain and lose friends so rapidly I could barely keep track of them. Who was speaking to me today? Who wasn't? Who loved us? Who remembered us? You pretended your friends were just like you, then BOOM!—they disappeared. I remember staring at a puddle of water after a thunderstorm, watching it evaporate, thinking, "Is this what people do?" The worst part was, I felt very attracted to words like "immortal," "eternal," and "forever." As the poet Peter Heitkamp has written, "Always is nice/to have, but it doesn't/last long."

Whenever I notice something out in public that has been lost, the famous single shoes scattered along highways, a child's hair clip or a tiny toy, I want an announcement made: *Here it is!*

Losing makes us miserable, startles us awake. It's also inevitable. Tom Clark has written, "There remains the problem of not being able to see one's loved ones again, up against the problem of never having seen them in the first place. Were they simply too close to be looked at?" Losing casts all kinds of shadows on what we thought we knew.

Is there anything good about losing? Does loss help us discover anything? Maybe sometimes we notice or take better care of what we still have. Momentarily. Maybe the reason we talk about our petty losses with such energy is that there are so many inevitable larger ones that can never be redeemed or reclaimed. The people. The eras of our lives. "All my life I have been waiting for this phone call," a grown friend said to me on the day his father died. No matter how many things we've lost already (few lines ring as familiar from the last century of American poetry as Elizabeth Bishop's "The art of losing isn't hard to master . . ."), we don't necessarily find losing any easier to heal from or to comprehend.

Once a class of unruly students came into sudden, clear focus when I entered their room and said simply, "What have you lost? Write it down." The lists were long and haunted. Freedom. Memory. Cats. Great-aunts. Being little. I remember more people turning over their papers to write on the backs that day than ever before. Everyone had lost so much already. Their poems were thoughtful, poignant ruminations, by far the best descriptive and narrative writing in our time together. I was reminded of something a teacher told us when I was in school: *The things that cause you friction are the things from which you might make art.* Surely losing is one of the most endemic frictions of our journey.

Besides writing legions of losing poems myself, feeling how many odd, angular ways the subject begins to creep into everything we say, I began looking for poems that express and explore experiences of loss. I kept files of them for years. They came to me for this book in many various ways. Envelopes from strangers. People I had met only once, who sent me sheaves of poems. Old friends sending messages for the first time in years. Magazines. Someone on an island.

Of course there are things we would like to lose—regret, worry, self-consciousness, frustration, envy, weight, fear. I have noticed it is harder to find poems written about those losses, though. And I have looked and looked. Maybe you will find them. Maybe you are writing one now.

Naomi Shibab Nye
San Antonio, Texas

Dedication

This is to poems that get
lost in the dark,

poems that flutter
away, white moths
just out of reach,
camouflaged against
rough plaster of
bedroom ceiling,
little bumps and
patterns of branches
cast by light from streetlamps,
neighbors' windows,
sometimes the
moon.

In that criss-crossed and
curtained glow
you only see them
when they move.
To grab is
to crush and keep
them earthbound, snow
of bitter wing dust on
your hands and
fingers,

fine as the powder of poems
lost in time, slipped
in among old papers
tossed away, whispers
that now annoy the hair on
the back of your head like a
strand of spider web
you brushed
one high school night,
still sticky with the first
line of your
first poem, caught,
then struggling free:

"Trees and shadows of
trees . . ."

Jim Natal

What the Stones Know

Fire says
"The flesh. The flesh."

Water says
"Hair."

The air says
one or two feathers in a field of wheat.

Earth says
"Sweat."

The mowing
dazzles with the shadows of passing clouds.

I say to my son,

"Write your name
on everything that's yours."

Robert Dana

Years of Solitude
from THE FLOOD

To the one who sets a second place at the table anyway.

To the one at the back of the empty bus.

To the ones who name each piece of stained glass projected on a white wall.

To anyone convinced that a monologue is a conversation with the past.

To the one who loses with the deck he marked.

To those who are destined to inherit the meek.

To us.

Dionisio D. Martínez

what have you lost?

Orange Juice

It was dark
when my father drank
orange juice from the container.
I would hear the creaking
of his footsteps
in the hallway
past my bedroom
and the suction
of the refrigerator door
give way to his private
love of sweets in
the quiet night.

I longed to know
the sweetness
of my father, and
would rise to meet him,
my feet bare
on the cold kitchen floor, and
listen for clues.

Lisa Ruth Shulman

The Wren

he was small not ready yet
frantic
under the hedge
I caught him took him home
my father wasn't sure
wild birds he said
we've tried so many times
but he ate
what we made for him
and in three days
could fly
around the living room
it's time my father said
you have to let him go

outside
he sat on my shoulder
I shook him off he flew
to a branch of the maple
perched there
silent
his little eyes
I was a child I called him
back he came
stood for a moment
on my finger
then gone
I felt the spring of his legs
all day

Barbara McCauley

4

My Father's Coat

My father's coat was made
of finest muscle. Fish-scales
were its lining;
from them, waterfalls
glistened. Rainbow trout
swam in the depths of its pockets
among twigs and polished stones.
Inside this coat, my father
was invisible. He became
the smell of wet leaves,
the smoke of campfires,
and when he wrapped me in his
sleeves, I stepped inside
the dark forest.

Susie Mee

David

Last fall you threw the softball in the gutter
just as Dad had called us into dinner. It's still
there. So's an old cat's cradle in the apple tree
twigs had tried and failed to tie
out of kite string.
A grubby balsam glider wing still sticks
in the rot of the roof's redwood shingles.

If what we do is what we are,
you're all over the place.
You said the chimney ate your plastic boomerang.
If what we do is who we are,
you're still home
here with us;
more than underground.

William I. Elliott

My Father in the Stacks

For hours in his study he'd disappear
into the private chambers of a story.
Walls within walls, his bookshelves
dwarfed me. His large oak desk
held the family photo, tall, straight stacks,
and the yellow plots of legal pads.
Sometimes he'd pass me a book
if my hands were clean.

I've grown tall like my father
wandering dark hours of the afternoon
in fields of print, rustling pages.
Back home at the university
where my father teaches, I walk
through the library on the seventh floor,
no call number in mind.
I turn the aisle and he is there.
In the silence of so many books,
we do not know what to say.
I forgive our unwritten lives,
the years we haven't read.
We pass each other, my hands are clean.

David Hassler

what
have
you lost?

Battleground State Park

My mother and father
sit on opposite sides
of the scarred green picnic table.
He serves the potato salad,
she stares, impassive as the monolith
of William Henry Harrison behind her.

I play tag
with my eight-year-old shadow
chasing myself
around the twisted trees.
From behind an oak
I study my mother's
high cheekbones,
her straight black hair.
She could be Tecumseh's sister . . .

I disregard the years of their births,
I want so much some reason
that can't be my fault
to account for her anger.

The Park Ranger told us
Tecumseh's body was never found.

The pitch of my mother's voice
frightens me, even in song,
but I want her to sing now,
some ancient Shawnee chant.
I want to vanish with her
into the woods, my father
calling after us
not *come back*
but *go.*

Of course our lives played out a different story,
but even now there are things I believe
are not impossible:

she could have been Tecumseh's great-granddaughter,
we could have been happy.

Martha Christina

what have you lost?

Nine

On his first day of baseball practice,
Benjamin says the other boys are all older
and bigger, and his mother snaps
You've never even met them.
What do you know about that?
He says to me later,
If she dies and my dad marries someone else
I can watch PG movies and get
a Nintendo.

The world is a dark place full of buzzards
and dead things, and he is too skinny, too short.
The boys down the street tie him to a tree
and throw Nerfballs at him,
then invite him over to watch dinosaur movies,
but Oh! The Misery, they are PG.

He sits in the top bunk late at night
all skinny elbows and knees,
big eyes, wide awake. *You can sleep*
in the bottom bunk, he says. *Please?*
He thinks about airplane crashes
and slow painful bacterial deaths
from picking up turtles and dead tadpoles
he found floating in the creek. He thinks about
eggs being chicken fetuses and millions of goldfish
floating belly up in the sewers underground, like April
and Junebug, and when he steps over grates,
he looks for a flash of gold, a silver fin.

He scratches his back with broken nails,
he chews his fingers. He wants a shirt that says
No Fear and one with holes and strings hanging down.
The last thing at night, before he crawls into the top bunk,
he kisses Hannah good-night. He hugs me.
He lingers in Christine's doorway,
a skinny blond question mark, plea for love.
But she is older now. She wears a training bra.
She has seen a world he will never know,
and he can't compete with her fearless wisdom.
Hey Chrissy! he says.
Hey Chrissy! Why won't you kiss me?

Amy Adams

Emergency Situation

I threw out your blue underwear,
Mother said. It had a hole in it.
No son of mine will ever be caught wearing that.
It's a reflection on me. It makes me look bad.
I know no one can see it. But you can't be sure.
Let's say you break your leg. You're rushed
to the hospital. The nurse takes off
your pants. She'll see it. The doctor
may not even put on a cast, because
he'll think you come from a poor family.
I didn't bring you up to embarrass me.
When you were little I dressed you up
as a girl. You were gorgeous.
You had curls hanging over your face.
But let's be honest. You're no longer cute.
You're too old to get away with anything.

Hal Sirowitz

The Ants Are Using Sticks for Walls

Ten-year-old girls want to be fourteen. When I was,
and Mother gave me stockings on Christmas eve,
my stomach shrunk, threw up the oyster stew.
Silk stockings and a garter belt. Grown up.
I wore them; every morning
she checked my legs for seams.
Grown up:
afternoon tea, old ladies, church ladies
asking me,
watching me, what I planned to do.

Hot. Too hot to breathe in air enough
to climb the canyon wall without stopping
to drink from the hidden spring,
seeping the weight of rain.
I held my thumbs in my palms, walked
around the rim, looked for the persons
Mother worried about, thought about what she thought
could be done with me if I went to school bare-legged.

I took the stockings off, buried them,
and waited for dark
to feel my way by yucca plants
aligned with the constellations.

Sandra Gail Teichmann

The Changeling

One day you see it so clearly.
You could not really be their child.
Your parents would know it,
if they could look inside you.
Despite what relatives say
about mother's nose or smile
or father's eyes and toes,
the mirror tells the truth;
you are different.

At first you try to hide the fact.
You are glad you have been taken in
and have a place to sleep,
and eat. But soon,
you no longer want their charity.
You see through their affection.
You hear the phony note
in the assurance that of course
you are theirs, of course
they love you. You know better.

You look for a likeness in the faces
of strangers. You search for kinship
in books. You look at maps
that can show you the way.
You definitely know you are not
meant to do what your mother does,
your father. Even your supposed siblings,
however friendly and familiar,

cannot understand what occupies
your heart. So you choose to sleep
under the bed or in the attic.
You wish you had been left
to be brought up by the wolves,
or that the floating city
will soon return to collect
its lost children. You want
your real parents to finally come,
clutching the worn and torn documents
from the orphanage, to embrace you
with tear-stained faces.

Meanwhile you wait,
preparing. You study
your chosen subject. You write
your poems. You feed
the original flame that burns
inside you, because you know
that is the only way
you will get to live the life
that is meant to be yours.

Siv Cedering

The Father, Who Could Not Swim

Morning was a mouthful of water
when I first learned of dying:
Kaufman's dad was fishing when he tipped
his aluminum boat. He never heard
the shouts that flattened
on the ripples above him; he was sinking
deep into the blue waltz
of the lake
(the way my father did
when he folded the newspaper filled with wars
in half, in half
again, then pressed his creased forehead
miles into his pillow).

Somewhere a knife shreds the night
like barracuda, a bullet punctures a quiet brain
like a sliver from a nightmare:
(whatever kills another man's flesh
numbs the skin on my father's wrist).

Still brushing my teeth before school,
I heard Dad's deep breaths
behind me. I knew he wanted
to rest his leaden palm on my shoulder,
but in the bathroom mirror I watched
his wavy reflection slowly turning,
the screen door closing behind him like an eyelid.

Bill Meissner

Son, Skating

He could be anybody's child—
spinning on the brightly lit ice.
He wears a uniform: ski cap,
a dark jacket over shirts
with the sleeves rolled up.
Here, he is one of a dozen,
fine-tuned, swift as knives.

Snow swarms in the headlights.
I am only a red car, a voice,
a *yes* or a *no*. His skates are more
than wings; he slips into the
envelope of his body, tall
and silent, no more mine
than he ever was.

Judith Kitchen

The New Blade

My son is using a new razor
with clumsy hands.
Grooming himself as a grownup for the first time,
he spreads his elbows wide, as in a ritual,
very fastidiously, not looking sideways.
From below his temple a smear of blood
as big as a bird's tongue keeps flowing,
no matter how often he wipes it off,
and he looks a little afraid.
What is hurt in him, I wonder.
His naked back is moistened, shining bright
like a tree trunk with its bark peeled off.

Although he doesn't seem to hear them,
birds are singing loud in unison
around the young tree trunks.
He doesn't seem to see it,
but the sea is rolling in the mirror.

Anzai Hitoshi
Translated from Japanese by Naoshi Koriyama and Edward Lueders

Teenagers

One day they disappear
into their rooms.
Doors and lips shut
and we become strangers
in our own home.

I pace the hall, hear whispers,
a code I knew but can't remember,
mouthed by mouths I taught to speak.

Years later the door opens.
I see faces I once held,
open as sunflowers in my hands. I see
familiar skin now stretched on long bodies
that move past me
glowing almost like pearls.

Pat Mora

Devotion

you find yourself alone
leftover moments   late
        listless afternoons
no one to argue or ask you questions
you get used to being alone

metronome days reiterate
insects that sing go to sleep underground
delinquent winds bluster wetly and cold
colors drip from the trees like rain

in the kitchen your mother worries at the stove
a sour steam heavy in the air
she demands to know what's in your pockets
"You keep your hands shoved deep in there
as if you had no hands"

she does not mention the absence in the house
a thousand tasks keep her mouth and fingers busy
"You look like a monster from a vampire movie"
so you go to the bathroom, paint wounds on your neck

sadness is a moat of dark water
        a tangle of briars no one can cross
sadness   a habit of sackcloth you wear
in devotion to the god of loss

Chris Pealer

Custody

Now that the bargaining is finally over
and our house divided into separate
camps, I wait for the girl who rages
in my closet, who plunders panties
and bras, steals sweaters, soap and comb,
who lures me to a mirror where she gleams
like a missile beside me, my face
splintered as shrapnel.

For her I grow smaller, sunken,
my bones lent to solder her shape,
my skin to cast her sharp blade of beauty.
Were there more to give now:
    a clump of hair
    a tooth
    a band of muscle taut as a noose
I would surrender, let her wave
her red flag of insult,
cross the battlement of my back,

    were she here
    were she here.

Jan Bailey

Mother's Day

I do not doubt you would have liked
one of those pretty mothers in the ads:
    complete with adoring husband and happy children.
She's always smiling, and if she cries at all
it is absent of lights and camera,
makeup washed from her face.

But since you were born of my womb, I should tell you:
ever since I was small like you
I wanted to be myself—and for a woman that's hard—
(even my Guardian Angel refused to watch over me
when she heard).

I cannot tell you that I know the road.
Often I lose my way
and my life has been a painful crossing
navigating reefs, in and out of storms,
refusing to listen to the ghostly sirens
who invite me into the past,
neither compass nor binnacle to show me the way.

But I advance,
go forward holding to the hope
of some distant port
where you, my children—I'm sure—
will pull in one day
after I've been lost at sea.

—to my children

Daisy Zamora
Translated from Spanish by Margaret Randall and Elinor Randall

Waking Instructions

Crawl ashore
to the damp beginning of day.

Forget before and after.

Allow yourself
to be spelled differently.

It will feel like falling.

It has waiting attached.

Emma Mellon

*what
have
you lost?*

Simple Song of Being Oneself

The ivy tells me: you'll never
be ivy. And the wind:
you won't be wind. And the sea:
you won't be sea.

Rags, rivers, bridal dawn
tell me: you won't be rag or river,
you won't be bridal dawn.

The anchor, the four of diamonds, the sofa bed
tell me: you won't be us,
you never have been.

And so say dream, arch, peninsula,
spiderweb, espresso machine.

The mirror says:
how can you be a mirror
if all you give back is your own image?

Things say: try to be yourself
without us.
Spare us your love.

Delicately I flee from everything.
I try to stay alone. I find
death, fear.

Vittorio Bodini

Translated from Italian by Ruth Feldman and Brian Swann

I Myself

I myself
met me face to face at a crossroads.
I saw in my face
a stubborn expression, and a hardness
in the eyes, like
a man who would stop at nothing.

The road was narrow, and I said to me:
"Stand aside, let
me pass,
for I have to get to such and such a place."

But I was weak, and my enemy
fell upon me with all the weight of my flesh,
and I was left defeated in the ditch.

That's the way it happened, and I never could
reach that place, and ever since
my body walks alone, getting lost,
distorting whatever plans I make.

Ángel González

Translated from Spanish by Steven Ford Brown and Gutierrez Revuelta

and sometimes i hear this song in my head

we have always heard music
found ways to smooth back the edges
of madness
stretched our voices
to the slap of oar against water
heard blues in the snap of cotton breaking
from stem
we always been a music
people
sometimes lost in a jungle of tears
but we keep finding our way back
to that
clearing
at the center
of our selves
where the trees still talk to us
and our tongues keep remembering the rhythm
of the words we forgot
swaying on the backs of buses
and in hot kitchens
crooning
in pool halls and shared bathrooms
yeah/we carving a heartspace
and staring down the darkness some call our future
and they saying it be just dope and more dope
and no hope

and they don't even see we all the time
standing in the middle of the trees
and steady singing
you can't
you can't
you can't
touch this

Harriet Jacobs

Shedding Skin

Pulling out of the old scarred skin
(old rough thing I don't need now
I strip off
slip out of
leave behind)

I slough off deadscales
flick skinflakes to the ground

Shedding toughness
peeling layers down
to vulnerable stuff

And I'm blinking off old eyelids
for a new way of seeing

By the rock I rub against
I'm going to be tender again

Harryette Mullen

what
have i
you lost?

Song of the Prodigal Son

Give me back the sun's din
the schoolroom door
In the end, let the summer blaze
into my stubborn eyes

I've walked so much
that zeal and snow
singe my traveler's eye
Wet my lips now
with my bathtub sponge
Give back to me
the rustle of green trees
and the sea of always.

Heberto Padilla

Translated from Spanish by Alastair Reid and Alexander Coleman

Aqueducts

I have carried water
to bed with me every night
since I was able to tip a cup
to my lips with my own small hands,
adopted a cup as my own
for years at a time until
it was broken or lost—
though it was not the cup that mattered
so much as the holding of water,
the water keeping watch over the night.

Two centuries back, my grandmother's ancestors
built the aqueducts in Turin, Italy.
My mother tells me this today,
and it is the only thing I know of them—
the family *Audo*—a line sunk
by the weight of my great grandfather
Grosso—a name as vast
and still as the bowl of a reservoir.
The names of my great grandparents—
Celestina, Anton—are as far back
as I can name, as my mother can name.
The stories come to me slowly, as water
struggling to pass through a dam.

I know a few small things—like switchbacking
up a hill: that Celestina came to America first,
her hands empty of pennies and English—
that my grandmother refuses to speak
her native tongue, does not speak at all
of her life before my grandfather, the war navigator,
the architect of her world, who washed over
her family name like a flood.

I imagine the aqueducts of Northern Italy—
pressed into the landscape by my family's hands,
climbing into the city like children
into laps, reaching for my grandmother's face
with small-boned hands: the hands my mother
used to raise me above her head, the hands
in which I carry water—holding it to my lips
in the dark, night after night.

Brittney Corrigan

Invisibility

We celebrate their days,
eat hot dogs, love baseball,
but they say we were born to weed,
change diapers, carry crates in the grey of dawn
while they sleep. Awake, they look at us without seeing.

We see ourselves clearly, know ourselves
precisely, without parades and picnics.
To survive, we must.

I'm one of the invisible living among the notable.
Day after day I hear doors shut,
stumble over slurs, and bump into the man
who nods yes, yes, but isn't listening.

Renato Rosaldo

Breath

The people I come from were thrown away
as if they were nothing, whatever they might have
said become stone, beyond human patience,
except for the songs. But what is their daily
breath against all the ardent, cunning
justifications for murder?

The stunned drone of grief becomes the fierce,
tender undertone that bears up the world,

steady as a river grinding soil out of stone.
I'm thirsty for words to join that song—
cupped hands at the spring, a cup of
rain passed hand to hand, rain pooled
on stone, a living jewel, a clear
lens trembling with our breath.

David Williams

Almost Evenly Divided

My life
almost evenly divided
17½ years Puertorican
20½ years New Yorker

I've lost
a land that felt mine
flamboyanes, canarias
going to the bank con papi
learning to cook like mami
las parrandas
the sun that warms up the chickens
el campo en Lajas
mi prima Adira
la vida lenta
ser mujer puertorriqueña
ser mujer puertorriqueña

Almost evenly divided
but half lost

Emma Suárez-Báez

At Home

Far is where I am near.
Far is where I live.
My house is in the far.
The night is still.
A dog barks from a farm.
A tiny dog not far below.
The bark is soft and small.
A lamp keeps the stars away.
If I go out there they are.

Linda Gregg

what have you found?

Child Proof

Watch a baby walk after a rain
Legs jammed apart
By that wad of diaper

A delicate muddy business
Flattening sodden monkey grass
Moist order of begonia beds

Fat arms bat at air
Gosling flippers imprinted with
Swan memories

Neither mom nor mud nor gravity
Have won yet

Child is proof
We come from somewhere else
Where everyone flies

Lisa Brandenburg

what have you lost?

Taking My Son to His First Day of Kindergarten

As the eight o'clock bell spills
its racket into this mild September,
it is I, not he, who hesitates
in the clamor toward the open doors,
who spots the little ruffian throwing rocks
at the Trash-Master by the swings,
who shyly searches for Room 106,
where Miss Wynn waits with the name tags.

The halls still gust and flow
with the rush of new dresses, the scent
of denim and sharpened pencils.
Eighth-graders arrange themselves
in groups to tower in their nonchalance,
eyeing each other like sprinters at the blocks.

Near 106, a bulletin board
declares "The Season of Changes"
above a paper grove of sugar maples.
He pulls me on, then runs ahead,
fearless, blameless, gone.

William Trowbridge

Bittersweet

In the valley of each August,
I laid a highway of school supplies
on my hardwood floor—paste after paper
after scissors after notebooks—
all after Green-and-Gold-Boxed Crayons:
sixty-four wickless candles, each
wrapped like a present to itself.

In school I studied
that tiered chorus of color,
eased out a single waxen staff,
pressed its point to the bare
sheet of newsprint spread
like a blank universe
across my desk; then I drew.

The rustling, scraping, coughing
class dimmed as I struggled
to form myself: narrow unknowing
thighs, red U
of my smile, blue marble eyes.
The heel of my hand skated
paper; pools of color appeared.

I could make beauty!
But with each rub
of crayon, those once perfect
points rounded to nubs . . .
the first regret
I knew. Sharpened
was never the same.

Bittersweet still remains,
though some of the colors
I loved are now gone: Blue-
gray, Raw Umber and Maize. Instead
new tints—Tickle Me Pink, Mauvelous,
Teal—are plied by waves
of smooth young hands.

Lavonne J. Adams

First Grade

Aftertaste of chocolate milk;
sleek sun dancing off windows;
the small paper clocks
we spent so many days on, fixing hands
with tacks, turning and turning them
to learn the names of the hours—

but none of the children's names comes back.
Not the boy with rumpled
black hair in front of me.
Not the girl with pale blue eyes
who raised her hand on every question.
Their faces I see clearly,

and the opened door
we longed each day to bolt through,
and the red and yellow cut-out paper leaves
about to blow away on the bulletin board.
But no names return, even if
I stare long into the line of faces.

And what about the teacher
who stayed only a year in our small town?
Dark-haired, quiet, always sad;
her husband off at war in another land.
Calm and younger in my mind, her face
reflects bronze light from the trees.

She looks up from her desk, about to speak,
to call on me with a question.
And did I know the answer?
And could I tell her now?

Roger Jones

The New World

Dark green burnished skin
covered his whole lean body.
That was all he was wearing, standing
on the front lawn of the Montclair Art Museum.
He was a young boy, probably about my age
when the sculptor had fashioned him.

I stood there staring between his legs.
A small limp stick resting on a sack of marbles
where a slit was supposed to be.
All the leaves in the large maples rustled
like a grandmother coming upstairs.

He seemed comfortable wearing only himself,
oblivious to my gaze. I suddenly saw
words go by in my head: *my father is*
like that, all the boys in my school are like that,
all the boys in my class standing right here!
How do they stand it?

My second grade teacher, Mrs. Lowe,
hurried us on. "Let's go inside, children,
so many wonderful pictures to see."

I dutifully stopped in front of all the paintings
and felt their colors wash over me, but what
I was really thinking about was outside:
just now, how I had divided in two.

Sandra Larson

The Forest of My Hair

I'm 28 years old in the flesh
but in a mirror all I can see
is a boy after his first crew cut,
five years old and wondering
what happened to his hair,

disbelieving it would ever
grow back, as the barber
and his grandfather promised,
while he wept, silently,
trembling air through his lips,
pointing at his hair
strewn across a tiled floor.

My grandfather unwrapped
sour balls for both of us, and,
leaving his Falcon behind,
walked with me to the woods.

These woods, he said, *are yours.*
They were mine, but I give them
to you. I am old, and it is only right
they should now belong to you.

I have lived most of my life
in the absence of that
gentle voice, and those
woods of mine were clear-cut
years ago, but my hair,
I wear it long in honor of him.

James Tolan

what have you lost?

43

Returning to the West: Mountain Legend

The mountain voice rises,
channels into valleys and between
our bodies. Our trail's fragile lines
are blown through dirt and rocks
and grass, blown beyond
what we can see.

The Papagos say the mountain
comes from ocean, parts the water
and turns around.
I don't know what that means.
The Papago woman says her heart
stands with the sea.
I could be that woman.

The language of air is in this wind
blowing from dust to cloud to rain.
Once I knew words that spoke
of rainbow moccasin strings
and white cloth over cactus ribs.
Now I know only the wind.

Denise Overfield

what have you lost?

Drifter, Owl, Mouse

It's a shame we have to train porpoises
to be like us. Rather we should be like them.
And take the great gray owl. I would
like to follow it. To take its picture.
Elusive and stately. That's how I want
to be. No prisoner to the earth, but
a sky-captain. That, too, is what I want to be.
Did anyone ever believe the mouse could
escape the owl? Did anyone ever believe
only men could love? I would like
to take a caterpillar and turn it inside out
like a sock. To see what's there. To see
why it takes such innocence to spin a cocoon.
What is said is not always what is heard.
Somewhere a mouse prays in an owl's beak:
there a drifter puts a hole in the owl's
head, the mouse a death within a death.
This is the world none of them wanted.

Ken Fontenot

Kind

I hadn't noticed
till a death took me outside
and left me there
that grass lifts so quietly
to catch everything
we drop and we drop
everything.

Leonard Nathan

Last-Minute Message for a Time Capsule

I have to tell you this, whoever you are:
that on one summer morning here, the ocean
pounded in on tumbledown breakers,
a south wind, bustling along the shore,
whipped the froth into little rainbows,
and a reckless gull swept down the beach
as if to fly were everything it needed.
I thought of your hovering saucers,
looking for clues, and I wanted to write this down,
so it wouldn't be lost forever—
that once upon a time we had
meadows here, and astonishing things,
swans and frogs and luna moths
and blue skies that could stagger your heart.
We could have had them still,
and welcomed you to earth, but
we also had the righteous ones
who worshipped the True Faith, and Holy War.
When you go home to your shining galaxy,
say that what you learned
from this dead and barren place is
to beware the righteous ones.

Philip Appleman

That Was the Summer We Had Animals

Everything then was a comfort.
The breeze we noticed was a small
song, a single draw across the leaves.

We slept, held in cotton bags, wrapped
in a fresh night.
We lay and felt the stars were common; they
were stars, wonderful—only stars.

Sometimes it
can be a sparrow hopping on my front step.
Another time, it can be a moment lost
to memory. Another, a child
walking. And then the hand.

Jack Ridl

*what
have i
you lost?*

Lens

I spend hours in my red room coaching myself.
Listening. Wondering why shouting explodes the house,
why table knives are different, drugs need to be hidden and
    Mom has to be watched.

Dad's long footsteps skip stairs to stop her. "It'll be better when
    I'm dead."
Dad grabs her arms, shakes her, says "Shut it off, shut it off."
I stare a deep hole into their backs.

Twenty years later, the photo album's acid-browned pages need
    replacement.
Photographs are loose in my hands—shuffle 1975, 73, 62, 81:
    put life
in chronological order, stagger the family under magnetized page,

Label the date in the margin: a journalist recording news. I close
    my eyes:
imagine it's only a movie. Her shrieks box my ears.
Like skin hurting, times I fall from my bicycle, hunks of ugly gravel

Burrow in elbows and knees. That night, bedtime snack, a scoop
    of ice cream
and a rotten banana. Photographs miss the truths we know.
"This stays in our family," she tells me, pulling the curling iron
    through her hair.

She can't leave without me! I want to die too. Mother applies
lipstick and eyeliner. We are close. I keep the secret
like a good spy would, clinging to the knowledge like a scab.

Ten calendars later, another attempt. Too many now to keep
    count.
At the emergency room Dad figures, "She slipped from the
    ladder
while cleaning windows with a razor." She had pleaded with
    him not to tell.

She's cut the middle of her arm. We decide the story is
    plausible. The hospital
smells astringent: stinging, like peroxide on open flesh. We wait
    in a sterile room.
On a shelf is a brown bottle labeled ALCOHOL in huge

White letters (if only everything had a label). The nurse asks,
    "How did this happen?"
We tell our lie. I hold my silence, unable to look anyone in the eye.
Images flash in my mind. I wish them away: they persist.

Mother spinning. A mustang kicking out of the barn, wild with
    desire.
Get out, get out is all she wants. She cuts her legs on the
    wooden door.
It gets so bad, someone has to destroy her.

Shot in the chest. Fast—not the way people are destroyed. Tonight,
there are new eyes on the photo album. People say, "It's so great
    your mom
saved this stuff" and "what a nice book." I agree. Slowly.

My gaze tips away. I hear sounds pictures cannot catalogue: car
    motor thrums
in the garage. She barely pauses to leave. A roar passes up the stairs
before the door slams shut. I wonder,

Is this my last glance of Mother? At home I check more
    pictures,
Trap them under a thin veneer. There is a picture of the three of us.
I am just a toddler. We look innocent and clean.

—*for Mom and Dad*

Kimberly J. Brown

what
have I
you lost?

Sudden

If it had been a heart attack, the newspaper
might have used the word *massive*,
    as if a mountain range
        had opened inside her, but instead

it used the word *suddenly*, a light coming on

in an empty room. The telephone

fell from my shoulder, a black parrot repeating
    something happened, something awful

    a sunday, dusky. If it had been

terminal, we could have cradled her
as she grew smaller, wiped her mouth,
    said goodbye. But it was

      sudden,

how overnight we could be orphaned
& the world become a bell we'd crawl inside
& the ringing all we'd eat.

Nick Flynn

Organdy Curtains, Window,
South Bank of the Ohio

I lived the whole time with my hands cupped to the
    open eye,
the light advancing like a flock of turkeys.
If the shadow of the catalpa touched

the sun wall of the house at 3:30
I waited several minutes
and entered behind it,
branching out slowly,

respectful of such a broad expanse of white, of silence,
the one small window, a mother's hand, that once,
at the curtain. I knew when to look head on,
when to squint. Things happened, beginning with her,

on a clothesline, flashes of this or that against the sky,
colors, faces, lips moving, snatches of faces—

Then suddenly no wind at all. Light hangs in the organdy,
south bank of the Ohio, I don't remember the year.
I can tell by the way my protective hands move
which eye is open, how vast the orphanage
of silence, how still
each blade of tall grass.
Once inside I am alone

briefly, hanging there,
in the light.

James Baker Hall

On the Suicide of a Young Boy I Did Not Know

What do I do with this grief
that is not mine, this story
that is not a story but a real
life abruptly gone? What do I do
with these images of a boy
I never saw who got the revolver
his careful father kept unloaded
by the bed, methodically loaded
the cylinder with a bullet, a blank,
a bullet, lay down on the cool green
sheets of his parents' bed, put
the barrel inside his small hot mouth
and pulled the trigger? I did not know
the boy. I only know today
he would have turned fourteen and
when my friend last spoke to him he was trying
to decide which movie to see for his birthday
and whether he wanted butter pecan or chocolate chip
ice-cream cake. I only know his father found
his body still warm, his mother
can't say anything except that she will never go back
into her bedroom, his brothers have stopped speaking
to anyone. What can I do with these details

that do not belong to me? Bake them into a cake
for the grieving family? Scrape the bowl clean
of the boy's shocked blood, his last surly words
to his father, last disappointing report card, his soft
brown hair on the green sheets his braces his birthday
his hand on the gun other hand on the pillow still bearing
the curve of his mother's head? They do not want
my cake. I have nothing to give them, no place
in their despair, no right to this poem. But
sorrow has no sense of propriety; it lodges
where it pleases, needs little to thrive,
and takes what it wants.

—*for Kaitlin and Jorie*

Jennifer Weinblatt

What Grandma Taught Her

She hates to be
somewhere without
something to do.
They are off petting
the animals that don't
have a real home.
When she gets like this
her hands and feet fidget
her mind wanders as far
as it can in all directions
and keeps looking back.
Give her a pen and paper
so she can quiet her mind
like her grandmother
would do during
church service.
She would write her name
over and over.
Grandma taught her this
when she was eight years old
right after her mother died.

Melissa A. Stephenson

Seeing for You

The leaves left at the tops of trees
sound like rain in the wind. November—
the sparrows play at being leaves,
the leaves at being birds.
I play at seeing for you
now that you play at being gone.

Linda Allardt

what
have
you lost?

Leaving the Light On

Returning home late one night
I realized I had no idea
who Mother and Father were.
So I climbed the spindly apple tree
wondering why darkness made me larger
and peered inside their room
listening first to one,
then the other, like oars
dipping in the darkness
towing the lighted window away.

They were explaining while they spoke
the simple names of things
through which the world fell through
confused: Mother, Father, Home;
offering directions
to each other
like polite strangers,
the ones who go on
when it's all done,
half-finished, just begun,
and they go on.

Jack Myers

what have you lost?

What We Want

The longer we look, the younger you get. At nine o'clock, we are crawling through the small town streets looking for a baby. Who could have curled up on a tree stump to sleep, who may have been devoured by dogs or the famous Belington buffalo. People on porches peer over the railings at us. Our throats grow numb with shouting; they are whispering about responsibility.

When you come back, we are all sorry: it's only ten; you're nine years old; to be gone twelve hours isn't really so long. So we laugh, and sit on the porch and drink beer until very late. After all, we all want our names called through the streets all evening; we all want to be lost, and looked for, and found again and welcomed home in the smoky darkness on any summer night.

—*to Paul*

Maggie Anderson

What Great Grief Has Made the Empress Mute
NY Times Headline

Because it was raining outside the palace
Because there was no rain in her vicinity

Because people kept asking her questions
Because nobody ever asked her anything

Because marriage robbed her of her mother
Because she lost her daughters to the same tradition

Because her son laughed when she opened her mouth
Because he never delighted in anything she said

Because romance carried the rose inside a fist
Because she hungered for the fragrance of the rose

Because the jewels of her life did not belong to her
Because the glow of gold and silk disguised her soul

Because nothing she could say could change the melted
    music of her space
Because the privilege of her misery was something she could
    not disgrace

Because no one could imagine reasons for her grief
Because her grief required no imagination

Because it was raining outside the palace
Because there was no rain in her vicinity

—dedicated to *The Empress Michiko*
and to *Janice Mirikitani*

June Jordan

Silence

When I was young, I tried to make friends with silence
and persuade him to reveal things to me.
Then I lost him, for years. Now he's back
in my waking from a nap into sudden afternoon,
and again in a meeting that drifts out a window.

I tell him, I have no time, I have things to do;
and I avoid him, going straight from work to friends.
How they fidget and prattle, botching our time!
I grant their uneasiness as my own, and say so.
They mumble me away, twiddling their swizzle sticks.

Can't they blow out, just jump in and roll?
I want to feel them alive. What are friends for?
I'm not about to shrug off back home, alone,
and have to brittle up against the silence
I am coming back to anyway.

Peter Sears

What Gets Lost/Lo Que Se Pierde

I keep translating *traduzco continuamente*
entre palabras words *que no son las mias*
into other words which are mine *de palabras a mis palabras.*
Y finalmente de quien es el texto?
Who do words belong to?
Del escritor o del traductor writer, translator
o de los idiomas or to language itself?
Traductores, somos fantasmas que viven
entre aquel mundo y el nuestro
translators are ghosts who live
in a limbo between two worlds
pero poco a poco me ocurre
que el problema no es cuestion
de lo que se pierde en traducion
the problem is not a question
of what gets lost in translation
sino but rather *lo que se pierde*
what gets lost
entre la ocurrencia—sea de amor o de agonia
between the happening of love or pain
y el hecho de que llega
a existir en palabras
and their coming into words.

Para nosotros todos, amantes, habladores
for lovers or users of words
el problema es este this is the difficulty—
lo que se pierde what gets lost
no es lo que se pierde en traducion sino
is not what gets lost in translation but more
what gets lost in language itself *lo que se pierde*
en el hecho en la lengua,
en la palabra misma.

Alastair Reid

Naming

Let me tell you this once
(I will not be able to say it again):
I have lost the meaning of words.
Heavy, they ripped away from the sounds,
fell into cracked ground. For weeks
I scratched but what I dug up was
bicycle spokes, black melon rinds,
a smashed doll face—it was not meaning.
I don't know what I am saying.

I exaggerate. Not everything is gone.
I still know perfectly what sugar means,
and pine needle. Laughter is more
of a problem. And yellow often slides,
a plate of butter in the sun.
The meaning of flower has gone entirely;
so has the meaning of love. Now it is safe
to say: I love you. Now it is true.

Nancy Mairs

The Higher Reaches

A man had less and less to say,
and said it better and better.

"Soon," he gloated, "I'll have
nothing to say, and I'll say it
perfectly."

Bruce Bennett

here yet be dragons

so many languages have fallen
off of the edge of the world
into the dragon's mouth. some

where there be monsters whose teeth
are sharp and sparkle with lost

people. lost poems. who
among us can imagine ourselves
unimagined? who

among us can speak with so fragile
tongue and remain proud?

Lucille Clifton

Learning Persian

A hibernating language
lying in the dark corners of my mind,
awakes slowly after a ten year sleep.

Naked,
bones creaking,
it crawls forward,
searching for lost pieces of clothing
in forgotten nooks and crannies.

Ragged and unkempt,
it finally tries to rise.
It ventures out
on a wave of words.

The world lies before it
waiting to be sung.

Reza Shirazi

what have you found?

Driving

Nothing will ever again
be my grandfather's Opel Coupe
smelling of Old Spice
swirling dust in the hills near Beirut.
I am a child
and my grandfather changes gears.
He buys me thyme
pies and we drive
to Jordan.

Haas H. Mroue

what
have I
you lost?

The Sparrow and the Crumb

A sparrow nears a crumb
of bread large enough
for two, lifts it
with a miniature pair of
vise grips and wings it
toward a secret you

will never know. The
day feels skinny. Why
should you care what
a sparrow does with
a crumb? Still you almost

believe the sparrow
will return to share
part of the crumb. But
your ear finds the other
voice that remembers
to say, "Fat chance!"

Nathan Spoon

Other Lives

You see them from train windows
in little towns, in those solitary lights
all across Nebraska, in the mysteries
of backyards outside cities—

a single face looking up,
blurred and still as a photograph.
They come to life quickly
in gas stations, overheard in diners,

loom and dwindle, families
from dreams like memories too
far back to hold. Driving by
you go out to all those strange

rooms, all those drawn shades,
those huddled taverns on the highway,
cars nosed-in so close they seem
to touch. And they always snap shut,

fall into the past forever, vast lives
over in an instant. You feed
on this shortness, this mystery
of nearness and regret—such lives

so brief you seem immortal;
and you feed, too, on that old hope—
dim as a half-remembered
phone number—that somewhere

people are as you were always
told they were—people who swim
in certainty, who believe, who age
with precision, growing gray like

actors in a high school play.

Vern Rutsala

Hitchhiker

Driving home tonight
I see a hitchhiker
at the end of town.
He sits on a lifetime
packed into his suitcase,
arm extended, thumb pointing south,
toward Mexico.
Where brazen glare of highway lights
ends, and I-40 continues on into endless
prairie, his life unravels
in wind I create as I pass,
a loose thread in darkness,
bit off from the rest, offering
frightening acts or accidental gifts.
Headlights spray across
fleeting outline of his figure—
    a loneliness
in the large black buttons of his overcoat,
    a homelessness
in the leather straps of his English suitcase,
    hard black coldness of coal
in his boots and a sad wisdom in his unshaven face.
He is the pupil
who has stayed after school
the rest of his life,
to write *loneliness* and *love*
on the darkness,
with the chalky pumice of his heart.

Jimmy Santiago Baca

The Family Car

When I was a kid we always had big cars:
Pontiacs, Buicks, an Oldsmobile Rocket.
Each year the bodies looked the same
but the grills got chromier and meaner looking.
With Father behind the wheel, Mother watching the road,
my brother and I assigned to our life-time seats in back,
our faces were painted on the toy windows.
In the hot Texas summers people walking in the filmy heat
seemed to float above the melting asphalt
while we cruised in air conditioning behind tinted glass.
It was quiet in there with the doors locked,
the windows sealed. From my seat in the right rear
I watched the world fan by.
This was life. This was certainty. This was big car roominess.

Tom Absher

I never saw the road between our
house and Grandma's.
By the time we hit the highway,
I'd be curled up, asleep on the back seat.
Mom would shake my arm to wake me
as our old station wagon pulled into the
makeshift dirt driveway.
Grandma's house was a mansion to me
through my groggy, half-opened eyes,
with stone porch steps
painted green,
hiding between the gardenia bushes.
Inside, the house was like a
Chinese herb shop,
dried shrimp smells dangling
between the ginseng tea and
sugared fruit.
Grandma used to give me pieces of
candy wrapped in rice paper that I called
Handi-wrap.
I'd suck on the jellied sweetness
until the wrapper melted away
just like the trees and telephone poles
between our house and Grandma's.
I sometimes think that if I
doze off in the car today,
I'll wake up in the old station wagon
almost there.

Donna Lee

So Far

notices   flutter
        from   telephone   poles
           until   they   fade

OUR SWEET TABBY   AFRAID OF EVERYTHING
BIG GRAY CAT   HE IS OUR ONLY CHILD
SIBERIAN HUSKY   NEEDS HIS MEDICINE
FEMALE SCHNAUZER   WE ARE SICK WITH WORRY

        all night I imagine their feet
          tapping up the sidewalk
      under the blooming crepe myrtle
        and the swoon of jasmine
             into the secret hedges
                  into the dark cool caves
           of the banana-palm grove
        and we cannot catch them
        or know what they are thinking
      when they go so far from home

OUR BELOVED TURTLE   RED DOT ON FOREHEAD
VEGETARIAN   NAME OF KALI

please please please
    if you see them
call me   call me   call me

Naomi Shihab Nye

Travelling Light

It's as though I saw it all
diminished to the core
the whole day to a minute
the suitcase to a book
the long conversation to a word
looks of longing to a smile
and hopeless choice to what must be
it is so light, so clear
I want nothing more anymore
 only wind stroking waves
 onto a distant shore

Kirsti Simonsuuri
Translated from Finnish by Jascha Kessler and Kirsti Simonsuuri

*what
have
you lost?*

Legend

Even while you were looking straight at me
you were always somewhere else, very far away.
I could never tell if you knew I was talking to you
or you just didn't want to hear me. You were that distant.

So when I turned my attention to the trees,
the air that brought me the trees, the stones
and everything I walked in and out of, you suddenly
began to speak to me. And your breath was so warm
and sweet that it took me very far away inside me
to a place where I was born, growing up before I was born.

Craig Czury

what have you found?

Stranded

I am so in love I can't find my hat.
I swallow fat happy drops of your name.
Your name is dripping from my eyelashes.

My name is the eyes of a kitten on the top branch.
My name is two Chinese men squatting
in a ruined guard station high at Badaling.
Someone once laid the first stone of my great wall.

Yesterday, my name was a ring of pollen fallen
from the deep center of a lily.

My name means *one who sleeps with
her eyes open.* I used to say
I was dreaming when they slid closed.
I've stopped pretending,
stare forward, backward.
I have been waiting so long.

My mother thinks my name is basil
thriving in the sun, ceiling fan stuck
on full speed, the persistence of mint.
In your dream my name is the leggy
avocado tree sprung overnight from
the firm shiny core you trusted.

I'm thinking of hot sand, thinking
of the exact spot stranded
between the protection of shade
and the salty thrill of waves.
I'm thinking of the moment
lost somewhere in between
when you decide to keep going.

Jenny Browne

Today I'll Sit Still

Today I'll sit still.
When my dog shuffles over and offers me
his fleas and his soul, I'll turn away.
To everything I'll close my eyes,
slice the darkness and eat it.
I'll refuse to give money on a platter
or a wet kiss under the moon.
Today I'll just sit
and say *No* to everyone and everything.
To the book on my desk, its sad tale
of abandonment, remorse and death;
I'll keep it on the tip of my tongue
like a lukewarm dime.
No to the daily mail with its greasy fingers,
no to the telephone and its humming
through the carcass of a sparrow,
no to every projection of the self.
No to me, this preposterous accident
who speaks of the "self."
Today I'll be anti-social.
Today I'll grow into myself, be the river
of my blood, the sky inside my eyes,
the maze of my ribs, the dust that settles
on my heart. I'll let my bones sink
like pebbles in a pond.
I'll let my feet grow roots and be an extra zero
on the checks that I'll refuse to write.

Ernesto Trejo

This Isn't Fair

I love you as my mother loves the orchid
my brother Rick brought her five years ago
that finally bloomed. Two beautiful flowers.
I love you as my brother Rick and I used to love

the robin eggs we collected in our childhood
that never hatched. Today when I asked you,
"Do you love me?" you got up from the chair
you were sitting in and walked out of the room.

I called you back, frantic, and when you returned
I gave you a poem that I had been writing
for you since last December. You read it slowly

and said something I didn't hear, then sat back down
in your wooden rocking chair, and smiled at me
strangely, as if I were a camera, or something.

Chris Mahon

Someone told me you were in love
with another, another man
and so I went to my room
and wrote that article
against the government
for which they then
put me into jail

Ernesto Cardenal
Translated from Spanish by Quincy Troupe and Sergio Mondragón

Insurance

Each passing bird's a bit of punctuation thrown through the air,
And here is morning, old grammarian, descending a stair.

Let the ocean nibble at its edges.
Let the great parentheses of trees press it into shape.

To understand chaos, be chaos.
Brightness gets out of its white chair.

We know what can undo us, and we keep it where
We can see it, but what of the distance

That darkens and fills with the second thoughts of starlight,
That hangs over us every night its opulent alternatives.

Broken necklace of light, protect us from our unadorned nature,
From the slow crumbling insurance of belief,

From the diminutions that revise us and revise us,
Describing the one true gesture that we know,

The one that says, as the ocean repeated a minute ago,
Build up an argument for your life phrase by phrase.

Love is in the rewrites.
Be slow.

Vickie Karp

What are friends for, my mother asks.
A duty undone, visit missed,
casserole unbaked for sick Jane.
Someone has just made her bitter.

Nothing. They are for nothing, friends,
I think. All they do in the end—
they *touch* you. They fill you like music.

Rosellen Brown

what
have
you lost
and found?

Going Home

I saw you in the airport today,
ten years younger.
I wondered about the possibility
of there being two of you
in this world, two people who
silently grow as they speak,
letting people think
they are still small and dark.
The heir to your childhood
sat between her father and me
on the plane.
She was, of course,
silent but iron-willed, like that mood
you have, but she spoke Spanish.

Then some men came and
talked to her father.
She moved to his lap
and the seat was empty.
A woman sat there,
but I didn't know her at all.

Ben Judson

That Kind of Marriage

He slept upstairs.
She slept down.
It was that kind of marriage.

There are photos of the courtship:
he, dressed to the nines
she, a dark-eyed beauty—
hands touching by a top-down roadster.

But by the child's time,
family love came down in
two distinct beams.

John Sangster

She had thought

it wouldn't always be like this,
this running and running, this always repeating

what she had just done; she had thought it would be
different, that she would smell

the coffee, smell the roses, smell the scent of hay;
she had thought it would be better, somehow,

that they wouldn't all be so needy—she needing him,
he needing her, both of them needing the work, the life,

the children needing *her* life; she had thought
there would be times they would say to her *you're okay,*

you're the best there is.

Phebe Davidson

Divorce

Woke up suddenly thinking I heard crying.
Rushed through the dark house.
Stopped, remembering. Stood looking
out at the bright moonlight on concrete.

Jack Gilbert

my lost father

see where he moves
he leaves a wake of tears
see in the path of his going
the banners of regret
see just above him the cloud
of welcome   see him rise
see him enter the company
of husbands   fathers   sons

Lucille Clifton

It Was Here—

It was here. Right here
beside the brook and the old rosebush.
A late spring this year, the roses are still pale,
almost like your cheek
the first morning beyond death.
But it's coming,
only the light, only the fragrance, only the pleasure
won't be coming.

But it was here,
it was an evening with a moon,
the brook trickling,
like now. Take my hand,
put your arm there.
And we'll set out
together in the summer night,
silently, toward
what isn't.

Rolf Jacobsen
Translated from Norwegian by Roger Greenwald

what have you lost?

Mindleaving

Mindleaving,
the son calls it, the way his father
is unable to distinguish the kitchen sink
from the refrigerator.
The way the faces of his children
are like birch leaves that drop to the sidewalk.
He talks about the crates
of pomegranates at Eastern Market.
But he was never there.
He forgets to eat;
undresses before a mirror in the dark
and knows how much he once weighed,
how much has departed his life.
Always amused that the Ford
parked in the driveway refuses to start,
he sits at the breakfast table each morning,
grateful once more for how cigarettes taste.
His son never says anything.
If he does, it is weather this and weather that.
The father sits stiff and thinks about it.
The clouds pass over.
The pussy willows sway back and forth.
The son says it looks like a downpour.
And then the downpour.

—*after Maxine Kumin and Greg Kuzma*

Hayan Charara

Shrink-wrapped

How did she arrive
at such a little life?
Where she spends several days
scheduling her book return to the library.

Where the crumbs on her kitchen counter
worry her for hours.
Where she won't wipe them up for fear
of losing something to do.

Where she creeps through every room
adjusting pictures a few millimeters,
until they're all slightly crooked.

Where she tears out
page after page in her journal,
because there is no one to see,
nothing to write.

Where the gas meter man
will knock repeatedly for days,
and she pretends not to hear.

Where the walls begin to bend
during certain rainy weeks,
making it impossible to breathe.

Where she eats the same meal
for three weeks running.
Where she never enters a bank.
Where she never learns to drive.

Where she never talks, not even to herself.
Where the herbs in her neighbor's garden
blacken from frost one morning,
so she hacks them to death
with his garden rake.

Where she obsesses over
airlock freezer bags,
their plastic sweetness,
their breathless perfection.

Or sheets of Saran Wrap,
the snapped invisibility;
how wonderful they feel
clinging wordless to her skin.

Until she's finally sealed
into this silent world,
spotless and magical,
shrinking forever
within her little life.

Carla Hartsfield

Where on This Earth

Where on this earth do we reach the ones who are gone?

Suddenly parted, does it matter to whisper their names over breakfast?

When we wake feeling the rearranged world they have left. Shall we imitate their laughter? Mulch the side yard's Sweet William and larkspur? Finish what they never did?

As leaves flicker at the window, morning light and memory soothing like a lullaby which is afterall a parting,

I think of her, standing in the kitchen to water the violets, and finally I dream if I miss her so much I should speak to her anyway.

What would you say if you could?

Can we write down the way hollyhocks stand in the garden now, how many cups are left from a Norwegian mother's steerage, how a child's face has changed and grown to its purpose among us?

The tiger lilies we water for the departed, the old mandolin played on the porch in the evening—do they do any good?

And the ones who go terribly, alone or burning—

can any hand we offer now comfort them?

With last things unsaid, is a ring or an apple tree given in love enough?

When the rain barrel is emptied, shall we stand in the door yard where they did the day they were young?

Where on this earth do we reach the ones who have left us?

—for Jim Moore

Patricia Kirkpatrick

Garage Sale

After she had
that last big
garage sale
she floated
off into
the sky

& I
heard her
say there was
nothing keeping
her here anymore

& I was much more
cautious about the stuff
I got rid of after that.

Brian Andreas

Words My Friend Can't Bring Himself to Say

Miss Betty showed us the game:
she'd cover her eyes and we'd find
the small places to hide.
We never understood that riddle
she sang as she searched under porches
and between stones.
But I remember how our knees
burned, arms wrapped around them,
making a tight ball.

So now, when I hear of her passing away
in a tiny house on the Vineyard,
I rush to count backwards from ten,
wondering why I hadn't looked for her sooner.

Quintin Prout

Journey

My father is looking at the end of his life
and it looks like the end of the world to him.
There is no one left from his town to say goodbye.
His childhood friends are saying
goodbye to their own lives.
He says he can see it coming,
the long trek into silence,
the idea of himself
seen through a distant lens—
a black figure disappearing into a tunnel of snow.
Wind enters his shoes, his mouth
with the sound of his heart
muffled in ice, buried
beneath the layers of fur
he's traveled with. All the things
he thought he couldn't live without.
A map, a compass, a pocket
watch and a scattering of coins
spray across the snow.
I am lightening my load,
so I will be ready
when the dogs lie down and die.
All day I hear him
making the necessary provisions.
Night whittles a sled of moon.
Shavings of wood
drift to the far
corners of the room.

Cathy Song

What Came to Me

I took the last
dusty piece of china
out of the barrel.
It was your gravy boat,
with a hard, brown
drop of gravy still
on the porcelain lip.
I grieved for you then
as I never had before.

Jane Kenyon

Benavides, Texas, 1906

No one lives in the town, except the grocer
who keeps the general store.

Each month, ranchers arrive for corn and beans,
sacks of flour, milled a county over.

A two-month-old paper, just arrived, translates, "War in
    Mexico."
For ranchers, the headlines read, "Expect Relatives."

Priests from the monastery ride through ten towns
to hear three weeks' confession and say Mass in the
    schoolhouse.

A photographer lines up families on front porches and yards;
one rancher includes his prize watermelons.

Marissa C. Martínez

what have you lost?

Letter to an Ancestor

What was it I always wanted to
know? Were you a sweet one to the
family? and did you sing to the
patch of weeds off your
front porch? Were the

dances like the ones we've
seen on television—and was that
enough to keep your blue eyes
bright and your forehead wrinkle-
free? Now that

I've found you in the
Census Book, I can't help but
wonder why we never heard a
word from out your way. I'd have
asked where you went on your
honeymoon. I'd have looked through
a thousand rotten records
to find the very mention of
your name.

Dwight Fullingim

The House
at 5 Allende Street

They've knocked down a colonial house at the center of the
    universe,
half a block from Tacuba Street, half a block from Donceles.

But this house returns at night
to be inhabited:
it still likes to hear my creaking
on the spiral staircase,
or the reverse:
it makes me listen to a dialogue of the ghosts,
in an unknown tongue.

Other times, I find myself at the center of the courtyard.
I look up:
the sun has stopped moving, at dusk.
A damp and ochre hour:
the color of the skin of the house.
Its breathing is the water spiraling over the bathtub drain.
There, in the bathroom, I can't see the bottom;
they say there's an iron staircase
that does not go all the way up to the top.
Upstairs, in the kitchen, the same:
the stairs don't go all the way down to the bottom.
It's the hour when the gods of the house appear:
my grandparents, whispering—I feel it—about some
    money-making business or other.
As if they'd stepped out of a photo album
I see them from a distance, blurry, almost motionless,
especially their sharp talons,
their thick lips.

Sepia glows in everything at this hour.
Night is a black angel that keeps coming down.
On the roof, however, there is a slow dripping.
In the pupils of the rain I am broken.
Here is where I lived the first instants of my life:
winter, 1953.

Now they're building a Banco de Comercio.
But I am still standing at the foot of the steep staircase
that leads to the sealed room
I've never seen.

Héctor Carreto
Translated from Spanish by Reginald Gibbons

Barns Collapsing

One leans into the wind
hung on a roofbeam and when
the wind stops folds into wood.
Another drops in a dry spell, boards shrunk.
After inspection I condemn
the empty fields, the sun and rain.
I examine each gulched board
in stalls left standing,
gaps in the boards gullies of light
before they're nailed up in restaurants and dens.

I investigate decay,
the lost shapes of things, rotten beams
burst open, license plates the color of dirt
nailed on the walls, and thumb-sized rusted bottlecaps.
Thirty year old hay spilling out of a barn.
Winch on a beam at the top sticking out.

A mile down the road a barn's about to go.
Huge thistles in the field behind it.
Wife works in town at the nursing home,
husband sits at the one kitchen window
in the grey barnlight caving in slowly.

John Vernon

Dream House

The logs are numbered before removal,
bright scrawls of blue chalk,
a children's hopscotch run amuck.
The tin roof's lifted off in two careful
pieces and somebody's dream house, circa
1910, is laid to rest, log by hand-adzed
log, in the back of a 4×4 pickup.
These beams that sheltered, raised
nine kids will be resurrected soon,
guest house, conversation piece.
If these walls could speak
I think you'd hear a moan, impossible to
translate into words and yet,
the meaning's clear, take me home. But

home's not where it was. The maple
trees are piled split wood
in what used to be my back yard,
4×4 in the drive, no bronze Bonneville,
no orange Cutlass. The waist-high pines
tower 40 feet now, even the mailbox is gone.
That huge expanse of lawn
where we played rollerbat is half the size
it used to be. Railroad tie steps
leading to the house are as shrunken,
splintered, as my memory of them.
How do I reconstruct these damaged scraps
of memory? And if we're moving back the clock,
can the door to my room, this time, lock?

Margo Solod

105

Small Town

The trains through our town
do not stop anymore.
When my father was a boy,
he would wait at the station
with my grandfather
to see them arrive.
Tall upon his father's shoulders,
he would peer into
each window and car
excited at the prospects
of what they might bring.
As the trains would pull away,
he would stand on the platform
watching as the train became
a small, black circle
then nothing.

From my porch, I can
see the tracks
hear the metallic grind of
the wheels as they
speed through our town;
whistle mocking, teasing.
Perhaps if we gather
where the station used to be
stand upon the weeded platform
sons raised to shoulders
as an offering,
brakes would squeal
doors would open
and the train would
share its stories
with a town too small to see.

Charles Owsley

What Was Once Reached For

The quiet old house we have come to sift through is for the
    first time cold.
I never remember the heat off, but now the window we open
    makes it
breezy enough to suck out the smells of pipe smoke and dog in
unvacuumed shag carpets, of shoe polish, dead posies and ashes.
On the hallway desk, the glass candy jar I used to reach for
preserves a cemented glob of sugared gumdrops, their colors
    dulled but primary.
In a back closet, stacks of boxed shoes sit in neat rows across
    the floor
like brick streets that, before asphalt, knew the weight of
    countless footsteps.
A charred briarwood pipe still holds strands of dried tobacco
on the bookshelf beside the easy chair, frayed and hard-worn.
A leash drapes over the brass coat hook behind the front door, a
black umbrella dangling from the doorknob like a dormant bat.
The silence and stillness aren't enough for us to know they're
    not here.
Only our even breathing makes noise, and only our shifting eyes
    move—
over empty vases, tea cups hanging in a glass cabinet,
    candlesticks
on the mantel flanking a faded portrait—as if we haven't seen
these things before, as if we didn't now own them.

Jeffrey Shotts

Father, Herald Me Home

I wind down
the streets bearing
nothing.
The sunlight casts refractions.
Its shadows
guard the outposts
through which I am winding homeward.

Father, sing me home.

I come emptyhanded
from other climates and chambers.
I have left my signed papers behind.

Father, sing me home.

Once I opened your lunch pail
and
shared the figs with you.
Once I removed your rainsoaked, mud-spattered boots.
Once my mother welcomed you home
with beans in pork, with coffee,
with a warm stove
to soften the tongues of your boots.

Father, sing me home.

Though I have no key, no magic, to bring to you,
reach across and pull me over the ravine.

Teresa Palomo Acosta

The Lost Glove Is Happy

Is it in the terminal I left
the brown, rabbit-fur-lined gloves
made in Taiwan? Gloves
I've worn in Ireland.
Gloves that kept my fingers
warm walking the bitter cold
coastline of Bull Island
with Howth and her necklace
of lights in the background.
Gloves lost now between Stillwater,
Oklahoma and Lubbock, Texas
on the way to see my mother.

Come, she said, I'm in
the midst of desolation. Come.
Take Southwest Airlines, past
Love Field. I'll be waiting
for you. I'll be waiting.

And in the mall, when I got
to Lubbock, arrived to embrace
my mother in desolation, she had
me strip, try on outfit
after outfit—sweaters, trousers,
skirts, shirts, shorts, slips
and blouses—to see like
Mary, Mary, quite contrary,
how does your garden, my garden,
grow? She in her mid-fifties

and I at the cliff-edge of
twenty-nine. My mother had me
fly to Lubbock and on the way

I lost my rabbit-
fur-lined gloves. When I got
there, when I arrived, when
I reached desolation, my mother
alone, in the middle of crazy
cottonfields, my mother in
desolation, I reached her,
I travelled to her,
to desolation, and in desolation
we were as lost as any
two mismatched gloves and
for a few moments we relaxed, lost
and strangely happy,
in the Lubbock Mall, without
labels stripped to our bones.

Nuala Archer

what have you lost?

A Serenade

Tapping me on the back, the night says,
"Don't stay home.
Go look for what you lost yesterday."
What I lost yesterday
resembles what I had lost the day before yesterday,
and what I lost the day before yesterday,
resembles what I had lost the day before that:

the backside of the board slipping down perpetually;
something that vanishes each time I go looking for it;
the nightly thirst while I'm walking along roads full of
      chuckholes
carrying an empty bag.

Perhaps it is something small.
Perhaps it is visible, perhaps invisible.
Perhaps it is something like a right.

I dream that the bag is too heavy for me to carry,
and when weightless morning comes I do it all over again.
Today I found
an utter stranger looking
for the same article that I had lost.

Sekine Hiroshi

Translated from Japanese by Naoshi Koriyama and Edward Lueders

A Game Nobody Won

In the jostle of the crowded train
I had my wallet picked.
I was mad at the loss of the wallet,
but I felt like laughing
at myself for being so mad.
I felt like soothing my foolishness,
saying, "Well, cool down, man."
The fact was, I didn't have much money
to keep in the wallet,
but my wallet was almost bursting
with all the name-cards of people.
By now the pickpocket in turn may be mad
at the wallet full of name-cards
instead of money,
looking foolish himself.
The guy may have stealthily tossed the wallet
out of the train window
over the railroad bridge.

Yamanoguchi Baku

Translated from Japanese by Naoshi Koriyama and Edward Lueders

My Grandmother Told Us Jokes

like the one about the man who
walked down the street
& turned into
a drugstore.

There was some secret in the moment
of that turning—when he was one thing,
became another—
that I return to again & again.

The day she stopped being
grandma and turned into
that madwoman.

The day my sister stopped being
& never came back. Perhaps there
was an instant between her sweet sleep

& the moment the fever struck,
from which she could have been plucked.

Do not make that turn, I want to say to the man
who becomes the drugstore; to the woman
who dies insane; to my sister;

to the boy who became an adult
the moment the cell door slammed shut.
I want to freeze-frame each instant of turning,

unfold in slow motion the moment of callous
change. Perhaps the secret's in the man's
intention; in the list in his pocket of mundane
nostrums he was sent to fetch home.

Or perhaps I've got it wrong,
perhaps there's a soda fountain where they all sit—
the man, my grandmother, my sister, the boy—

& drink nickel root beer floats, look back
on that fateful turn, & laugh among themselves
at the rest of us, who took it all so seriously.

Richard Beban

The Mentalist Leaves the Stage

In the huge applause, he palms the cards,
smiling, but frowning a little, too,
now shaking his head as though something's wrong,

as if suddenly the trick's up and he sees
the inspection number in the vest pocket
of the ugliest man in the audience,

the cameraman's final notice, the years
left in the stage manager's lungs,
sees where next year's mugger will hide

his wallet, his children's smallest
secrets, sees his wife reach
in her purse, dial the number that changes

everything—sees the cards already
cut and nothing left. He's looking
around, as if to be rid of his gift,

to wish it on anyone—the accountant
alone in the back row, maybe, a script girl,
the page taking his arm. But he's

old news, they're watching the next performer.
And a taxi's waiting. He sees its sprung
seat, the battery running low.

Memye Curtis Tucker

Part

Always someone's leaving for good. Easy to
say. Open a window. Leave
a note beside the typewriter—who reads it

standing there wants a moment alone
to consider the current of
the words. What's done, is. Are there

apologies musty in an overcoat, creased into
a pocketbook? I imagine
hesitations over the phone. *I didn't want*

to go. I had to. Simple, like water runs cool
down this blue-green glass.
Always someone's on the way out. You?

—*for Tiberiu Rus*

Steve Wilson

*what
have I
you lost?*

Plum Trees

There are no seasons in California,
just two plum trees
in my backyard.
All winter,
bare and knotted
like my mother's hands,
nails unpolished,
no wedding band.
In spring,
they bloom into
teenaged girls
who pull snowy slips
over their heads.
They are the daughters I may never have.
Come June,
they throw temper tantrums,
toss ripe, purple fruit
to the ground.
I don't mind.
I pick up after them,
an exasperated housewife
gathering strewn, dirty clothes
for another load of laundry,
but humming
all the while.

Later,
I turn the shiny pages of magazines,
tear out recipes
for pudding,
tortes,
jam.
Anything,
I think,
anything
to make good use
of plums.

Alison Seevak

Work

A man with the name Angel sewn on his shirt stands glumly
behind a checkout counter at the hardware store. His register is jammed.
Three or four of us standing in line shift from one foot to the other.
We toy with wing nuts on display and watch Angel angrily
because we're hungry and his register is jammed.
Angel is waiting for a manager to free him from this frozen instant
in the great river of commerce. He grips the sides of his register
as if they were the shoulders of a child and stares off above our heads
to the ceiling fan display and beyond. He must have family at home,
works two jobs probably, never quite sleeps enough.
The nature of work is so diminished.

When I think of work, I think of my immigrant grandfather and
    great uncle
pulling nails out of boards with their teeth. That was sport to them.
They elbowed their way through the railyards of Oklahoma, strapping
Russian Jews, pitting muscle against the dangers of the oilfields.
Or Fred Sims. I worked with him summers giving him the chance
to swing I-beams within inches of my head to keep me in my place.

Did I almost hit you, honey? he asked one or two beats late in
    that high-pitched voice of his.
Fred Sims, who laid railroad track through the Rockies, talked
of nights spent among mountain lions.
The dignity of pure labor. Of sweat.
His black arms at 70 as taut, lean and steely as a young
    middleweight's.

There are no standards to go by.
Work now means Angel standing sad-faced waiting for the
    register to unjam.
No measures. No depth. No wilderness inside us
that we have to wear down with hard labor.
Just the dull slide to oblivion.
No feral eyes tracking the night. No living on instinct.
No fox tip-toeing its way through the heart. No measure of us
    beyond ourselves.
Nothing left to tame.

Geoff Rips

Sister

you will arrive

at a point
when you realize
that you have been missing
from most of your life

you will forget
the redness of your mother's lips
but remember losing
a slice of skin on your knee

childhood will not pass quickly,
it will erode like paint around a doorknob

you will search
 the curve of your spine
 the knot in your stomach
 the seam of your dress

between temples, lips, legs

and you will find
pieces that fit together
and pieces
that aren't there

someone took them from you
without the permission
you did not know you had

you will glue the pieces together
and the cracks will leak
you will break open
fall apart
and I will help you
find you

we will wait till May
and dig a hole together
bury the pieces you have
and don't have

and I will lie
next to you
on the ground
until you grow

Andy Young

what have you found?

The Question

"We are what is missing from the world"
—Fernando Pessoa

Some questions have no answer.
Raised, they hang there in the mind
Like open mouths, full of something missing.
The great Portuguese poet, Pessoa,
Said that the idea of happiness
Is what makes men permanently sad.
The body, imagining the soul,
Looks ugly to itself.
A man hears a word, and the world
Becomes a place that he misunderstands.
So he climbs high into his life,
Ashamed of all he doesn't know,
And refuses to come down.

If you could coax him out again,
You could tell him, say,
That anything can be explained.
The shape of apples, for example,
By their love of travel.
Or that the sky is blue because
It's an easy color on the eyes.

*what
have I
you lost?*

Even the dog, chasing its tail,
Has, temporarily, a center.
Even the bird, disappearing into his hole
Knows that the world goes on without it.
And Pessoa, that eminently healthy man,
That artist, wore a blue wool hat
Even on the hottest summer days.
Simply to toss at strangers in the street.
He liked to see them catch it,
And grow immediately less strange.

Tony Hoagland

My Valhalla

Forget The Museum of Natural History,
The Metropolitan or The Smithsonian.
The collection I want to wander in
I call The Valhalla of Lost Things.

The Venus de Milo's arms are here,
she's grown quite attached to them.
I circle Leonardo's sixteen-foot-tall
equestrian statue, never cast, browse

all five-hundred-thousand volumes
of The Alexandrian Library, handle
artifacts of Atlantis. Here are all
the ballades and rondeaux of Villon,

the finished score of *The Unfinished
Symphony*, I read all of *Edwin Drood*
and *Answered Prayers*. I'll screen ten
missing reels of Von Stroheim's *Greed*,

hear the famous gap in Nixon's tapes.
There are lost things here so lost,
no one knows they were lost—manuscripts
by the unknown Kafka, far greater

than Kafka's; his best friend obeyed,
shredded every sheet. The cure for cancer
is here: The inventor didn't recognize,
the potion went unpatented . . .

In my museum no guard shushes me
for talking, there are no closing times,
it's always free. Here I can see
what no one living has seen, I satisfy

that within me which is not whole.
Here I am curator not of what is,
but of what should have been,
and what should be.

Robert Phillips

The Colors of Another Home

In the charged moment when the scarecrow raised
his shimmering arms, tossing the crows
into violent light,
a voice said clearly:
Sink deeper into the world.
The reeds swayed. I felt
the flesh of my palm tingle,
heard the crunch of gravel
under my sandal,
like the cracking of pond ice,
as slowly the very landscape echoed
and became familiar:
This is called déjà vu—

Then I saw myself
under the regression
a woman bending over a pond
in the fifteenth century, a feudal lord
drowning in a boat:

And my soul whispered
I am Japanese
—these mountain blues, these mute, cool greens
the colors of another home.

Cyrus Cassells

Fame

Fame does not care for one who wants it.
This small laurel leaf
Came years late.
When I desired it
So I could be loved
By a woman with violet lips
It eluded me again and again
And comes to me now that I am old,
Now that it does me no good.

Now that it does me no good
They throw it in my face
Almost
      like
          a
            shovelful
                  of
                      dirt . . .

Nicanor Parra

Translated from Spanish by Willis Barnstone

Tutu on the Curb

Tutu standing on the corner,
she look so nice!
Her hair all pin up in one bun,
one huge red hibiscus hanging out
over her right ear,
her blue Hawaiian print muumuu
blowing in the wind
as one bus driver blows one huge cloud
of smoke around her,
no wonder her hair so grey!
She squint and wiggle her nose
at the heat
and the thick stink fumes
the bus driver just futted all over her.
You can see her shrivel up
and shrink a little bit more.
Pretty soon, she going disappear
from the curb
forever.

Eric Chock

Passing Necessity

When I hear the first few bars of Vivaldi's
Mandolin Concerto, I am humbled
like the women on their knees at the Cathedral,
who light a chord of candles to San Antonio,
the Saint of things mislaid.

One summer when I thought I'd die of sadness—
I met a man who loved the Concerti Madrigalesco
and so we thought we'd found the cure for grief.
Buoyed in imitation—we dipped and rose, resting
briefly in each other's L'Inquietudine—as though
the notes lived on inside us, as though our half
and fractured songs had been made whole. We lived
as though the music could restore what we thought
we'd lost. But our Saint failed us.

Now I waken rinsed in baroque longing—to braid
my hair with violins. I hear a score of morning
greening through the trees, or fading summer
blued by a north wind. These are my Concerti:
L'Amoroso and La Notte, and anything made sweet
by flute or mandolin or real by absence.

Camille Domangue

Any Morning

Just lying on the couch and being happy.
Only humming a little, the quiet sound in the head.
Trouble is busy elsewhere at the moment, it has
so much to do in the world.

People who might judge are mostly asleep; they can't
monitor you all the time, and sometimes they forget.
When dawn flows over the hedge you can
get up and act busy.

Little corners like this, pieces of Heaven
left lying around, can be picked up and saved.
People won't even see that you have them,
they are so light and easy to hide.

Later in the day you can act like the others.
You can shake your head. You can frown.

William Stafford

what have you found?

Tough Ride

You smacked my five-year-old son on
the head, hissed, *Eat your beans*. You
set your watch on the table, *Five minutes
to clean your plate*. My hands shook.
You glared, dared me to defy. My bowels
seized. I ran to the bathroom. You rapped
your knuckles again on the child's skull. I froze.

David gulps his food down, swallows it
whole, chokes on it today. He thinks you're
the reason. He was forty, Monday; we talked.
He said, *Dad always clunked me on the head*.

Once I challenged your behavior. I was doing
dishes. You threw each plate against the wall.
China smashed until the dish drainer was empty.
That'll give you something to think about.

Tough sledding; I'm glad you're dead.

Mary Ann Wehler

Unveiling the Vietnam Memorial

In the failing light, survivors
found the name they sought
cut in the polished stone
and they stroked it
as if it were a person.
I watched on television,
far from that monument, far
from your grave.
If I do nothing
to release myself from this pain,
I will never forget you.
In the village of my body,
I, too, am a burn victim,
draped in wet skin.
And I will be buried as you were,
unhealed, as were the others—
Americans and Vietnamese.

Remember our dog?
She rolled in feathers, in leaves,
even dried turds—anything
to disguise herself, to stalk her prey.
How did we learn
to make a monument to some
and to call others enemy,

to conceal our species from itself?
With the body of each warrior
we place in the earth,
we etch ourselves most truly
into the cold memory of stone: the acid
history of our kind, which murders its own.

Fran Castan

Thinking of What the Jury Is Deliberating

I bet your grandmother made you cookies
when you'd stay over for the weekend,
and she'd smile even when you'd color the sun black.

Actually, I bet it was yellow or orange,
that you loved the monkey bars,
holding on, reaching for the next one.

I know your mother patched
you back together
when you tore your jeans playing.

Somehow, if these women weren't
so important, it would make it easier
to understand, if they'd been killed in a car accident
when you were 13, if your father had taken years
to grieve and left you with a television babysitter.

But there are all those anniversary pictures.

There is also the standard prom picture,
with the out-of-date pastel tuxedo,
followed by the stern boot training photo.

You wanted to be in the 82nd Airborne.
Had you not wanted to be the best,
it would be easier to understand.

Thinking about the jury deliberating,
my verdict is I'd like you to sit in a cell the rest of your life,
the faces of those you killed papering your wall,
explaining to your mother on each of her visits
how you could drive that Ryder truck.

Mick Hatten

I Give You Back

I release you, my beautiful and terrible
fear. I release you. You were my beloved
and hated twin, but now, I don't know you
as myself. I release you with all the
pain I would know at the death of
my children.

You are not my blood anymore.

I give you back to the soldiers
who burned down my home, beheaded my children,
raped and sodomized my brothers and sisters.
I give you back to those who stole the
food from our plates when we were starving.

I release you, fear, so you can no longer
keep me naked and frozen in the winter,
or smothered under blankets in the summer.

I release you
I release you
I release you
I release you

I am not afraid to be angry.
I am not afraid to rejoice.
I am not afraid to be black.
I am not afraid to be white.
I am not afraid to be hungry.
I am not afraid to be full.
I am not afraid to be hated.
I am not afraid to be loved.

To be loved, to be loved, fear.

Oh, you have choked me, but I gave you the leash.
You have gutted me but I gave you the knife.
You have devoured me, but I laid myself across the fire.

I take myself back, fear.
You are not my shadow any longer.
I won't hold you in my hands.
You can't live in my eyes, my ears, my voice
my belly, or in my heart my heart
my heart   my heart

But come here, fear
I am alive and you are so afraid
of dying.

Joy Harjo

Food. Music. Memory.

She says: Cupcakes. Brownies. Pies. She says:
Remember this. Bread. Stew. Sauce. She says:
All that time. She says: Singing. All I taught
you. She says: Crayon. Alligator. Boy Scouts.
She says: Baseball. Soccer. Track. She says:
I was there. Remember?

I say: Shouting. Silence. Shouting. I say:
Remember this. Scotch. Vodka. Kahlua. I say:
Cupcake. Meatloaf. Sauce. I say: Singing. All
you would not tell me. I say: Crayon. Dancing.
Guitar. I say: Belt. Hairbrush. Hand. I say:
I was there. Remember?

Susan Marie Scavo

*what
have
you lost?*

The Memory Prayer

I learned to breathe this way
when I left that body made of ashes,
river water, copal and huisache flowers.

When my breath was South
it was a feather as big as a palm frond.
The infinite miles were numbered in stars
and the earth was lit from inside.

My eyes were mirrors, my heart was wind.
The ground pulled my songs like a magnet.

The bananas were so ripe they spread like butter
when they first brought guns into the garden.

Our legacy is papaya, is frijól,
is sangria by the gallons.

Helix inside of helix, the color of blood.
Dead uncles. Lost friends. Forgotten íntimos.

For five hundred years of impossible weather,
this lightning has smelled like night,
weaving its net of forgetting across these lands.

John Phillip Santos

Raised Voices

I am so glad when you call, even with news
of chaos. Your voice spreads out across the night

and into all the years we did not talk,
into cold corners which bear no tracks
of the voice remembered. You tread so surely
where no family has gone before.
I hope you hear the warmth in my welcome.
It's time we had company by the fire.

In our house we avoided words that weren't nice.
I whispered them to azaleas and calla lilies
while you went off with boys in bluejeans and Chevys.
Daddy took me fishing when Mother insisted,
they gave you a phone when you cried
and after that your tears and stories

were for unseen friends. My best one
moved away just before you did.
My body changed the year you left
but the quiet remained the same, for six
more years it remained. We went
our ways as refugees. You raised children

and peas on a delta farm, I stayed in hiding
raising skin cancers and geraniums.
Finally we talked on couches in measured tones,
I started first to ask the questions,
now your voice has come to you—
ask me your questions.

We were raised in the same silence
and I am so glad when you call.

—for my sister

Jack Brannon

Lament

When the whippoorwill cries.
When the stars shine at dusk.
When the flies swarm on the kitchen screen.
When the house cat breathes in the baby's face.
When every autumn dead crickets, dead spiders,
the horned toad spitting blood
Blessed are the dead the rain falls on.
Sing of scorpions, of freight trains.
Sing of the cold, cold river,
where the current carried you away
in a cypress tree cradle.
Sing of cornstalks and bedsheets
and drawers full of maps,
of untouched coins and doorknobs
and the supper table.
Sing now like the crazy, black grackles
with their oily, black feathers,
who rise up all at once to fly
in some strange direction
turning the sky dark.
Sing like the little, brown sparrow.
Sing to me now if you can,
through a sky gone dark.

Catherine Bowman

Model of the Heart at the Franklin Institute

Once, as a child, I walked inside
that huge heart and touched its walls,
cool plastic curve of vein and artery,
clear colors of kindergarten art:
pink, red, blue. Sound curled close
to my small head, beat of blood
like waves saying and saying
a word I did not understand.
Alone, I missed my friend
with her laughing hands, listened
and touched so I could tell her
this was inside us, color
and song, muscle moving constant
blood along its highways. I did not know

how, much later, she would
die, her own heart shuddering
silent like a landscape after rain,
or how I would live, careful,
forgetting her fine hair and the way
I stood inside that sound, those colors
we might have painted on white paper
and hung to dry: a pink flower,
red house, a longing blue sky.

Kasey Jueds

145

Each Night

Images,
dream news,
fragments,
flash
then fade.
These darkened walls.

Here, I say.
Climb into
this story.
Be remembered!

Jay Bremyer

what
have i
you lost?

Waking Up in the Morning

Waking up in the morning
my unshaven cheek feels against the back of my hand
as if time, having eaten up another twenty-four of my hours,
left the crumbs on my face.

Zymunt Frankel

what have you lost?

Truth

Mine has always been a silent world.
So words have not been easy.
And words have been easy.
As easy as words.
As another lie; oh, I have lied.
And I have denied.
And then denied that I denied.
I have invented myself so many times
so that others would believe I was who they thought
I was, and I suppose, so that I, too, would believe.
And also for no particular reason.
Oh, I have lied.
And that is the truth.

Leroy V. Quintana

Regrets on the Way to an Airport

I never filled my suitcase with the remnants of the sky,
Nor forgave the naked onion because it made me cry,
Nor clothed the new-born desert with the birth mark in my eye,
Nor raised a thousand voices with the stillness of my sigh.
It's not because I couldn't but because I didn't try.

Ali Abunimah

Processes

Ten years ago
I was writing poems
brief as bird tracks.

A wing
encapsuled an entire spring.

Three morning grace notes
scored all summer.

A single beak
bit off autumn like a worm.

A few hieroglyphs
on the snow
said everything there was
to know of winter.

I was younger then.
I was more certain.

All my short spare poems
knotted themselves into a final word
like a crow shot from a tree.

But I've lost that brevity,
that arrogance
of what is what,
and my poems
flock like blackbirds
gleaning word after word,
line after line
from the waving field.

They are still famished,
cawing terribly in my mind.
I don't know what to give them.
I keep on writing.
and writing.

Joan Colby

Ghazal (For William Stafford)

I will follow my master and in the soft quiet
become a morning poet.

Listening to the world, all its questions
between today and tomorrow.

For a match starts a fire, a shout to a mountain
sometimes starts an avalanche.

The grey line of the road ahead embraces us;
yet we can still be lost in our own life.

When many people offer to be your guide,
perhaps it is because your father couldn't reach you.

David Keefe

Autumn Quince

How sad they are,
the promises we never return to.
They stay in our mouths,
roughen the tongue, lead lives of their own.
Houses built and unwittingly lived in;
a succession of milk bottles brought to the door
every morning and taken inside.

And which piece is real?
The music in the composer's ear
or the lapsed one the orchestra plays?
The world is a blurred version of itself—
marred, lovely, and flawed.
It is enough.

Jane Hirshfield

Cannon Beach

A gull overhead
like a comma. I pause

to listen for what
I think I ought to hear

in the pulse of ocean
on sand on sand

the sea like a hand
reaching out, drawing in

the things it leaves
for us, and takes

like you, standing beside me
smooth and purpled

as a boneshell
as if, all this time,

you were just waiting
to be found.

Susan V. Meyers

Christmas

I always feel that
the letter slipped into the mailbox
will never reach its destination
The bicycle parked by the side of the street
will be stolen by someone
The pressure cooker in my hands
will immediately explode
The TV broadcasting the soccer match
will break down
If I bump into something
Of course I get a concussion
If she doesn't come on this bus
I'll be left alone in this world

Why should a mature man bear
such heavy burdens
on his shoulders?

Lan Se

Translated from Chinese by John Rosenwald

Avalanche

This is the snow belt.
This is the snow that falls
fretful as the flicker
of our eyes when we dream.
This is where people ache
along the road in their vehicles,
cursing each and every member
of the road crew
by name. This is the pin oak
in the front lawn shivering
all night, and sometimes
all day. This is the habit
of watching clouds
throughout the afternoon,
hoping it'll hold off
till we make it home.
This is the trickle of water
in the bathroom and kitchen
to keep the pipes from freezing.
This is the shucking sound
of neighbors out with their snow
shovels, people so thick
with clothing, and still
so cold. This is day after day
of school cancellations, and hoping
for once it would never end.

This is the old man
who sees angels dying
with the weather, and the old woman
who keeps putting him back to bed.
This is the joy of stillness,
and the sadness of solitude.
This is the snow belt.
This is the belief
that everything has a reason,
even the tiny pain
that creeps through our shoes
and into our toes.

David B. Prather

Year's End

Now the seasons are closing their files
on each of us, the heavy drawers
full of certificates rolling back
into the tree trunks, a few old papers
flocking away. Someone we loved
has fallen from our thoughts,
making a little, glittering splash
like a bicycle pushed by a breeze.
Otherwise, not much has happened;
we fell in love again, finding
that one red feather on the wind.

Ted Kooser

How Forgetting Works in Late Winter

Fog thrown over house and pines, flimsy comforter.
Under the pines, mounds of snow exhaling. There
is my son who kicks the rotting cold, punches holes
in the snow's breath. Over his head the sun is a white hole,

and he scares a pine dove into it. Night-frost spines
my window. In the fire-grate, ash swirls, a flock
of gray wings. The air near me is so still

it's childless: a room where fever finishes its work
under the sheet. I finger the ache between eye and ear—
I run a hand through graying hair, like the boy runs out there.

My father was stationed at a window cold as this. Behind
his father's house, a hill of frost and brier: doves hunched
on iron spears fencing the family graves. I ran at them
waving hard. I made small clouds of breathlessness.

Robert Hill Long

Secret of Life

Once during the war
on a bus going to Portsmouth
a navy yard worker
told me the secret of life.

The secret of life, he said,
can never be passed down
one generation to the other.

The secret of life, he said,
is hunger. It makes an open hand.

The secret of life is money.
But only the small coins.

The secret of life, he said,
is love. You become what you lose.

The secret of life, he said,
is water. The world will end
in flood.

The secret of life, he said,
is circumstance.

If you catch the right bus
at the right time
you will sit next
to the secret teller

who will whisper it
in your ear.

Diana Der-Hovanessian

Tune

He went from us into
a humus, a silence clotted
in the duff between brush maples. He whistled

with his tongue against his teeth. We play the martial
overture he loved and joke about how easily
his eyes would fill with tears. He never fit

the wicker sofa. His summer beard had rogue
red-gold among the white. Reclining
on the porch he would tilt up

to hear the windchime describing secret
stanzas of the breeze. Its circles of flaked
shell were like his bones. We carried lunch

out to him, squatted near the chair
to kiss the knobs and rivers of his hands.
The dog that had survived distemper licked

a soggy patch around the knee of his seersucker
pants. And then transparency,
which had been lapping at him, closed

over his place. In the last years
he had not laughed or written. But now, again,
we open drawers to find his midnight

carbons, his rustling onionskin—now we listen
for the faint syncopation
of a typewriter from an upstairs room.

what have you found?

Frances Richard

Something I Remember

I used to live on the 18th floor
of an apartment building on the Lower East Side.
Spent a lot of time waiting
for the elevator to take me down.

What I liked best were buses and subways.
The Avenue D bus took me to school,
to Rachel's house, and all the way cross town.
The subway took me anywhere and fast.

My father is still up there, looking out
over the East River, watering his plants.
He wants me to tell him something I remember
that would prove his goodness.

I see his trees rooting in big pots
18 floors above the concrete
of Manhattan. I could tell him that
before he dies. Maybe he won't notice
he's not in the picture. I could tell him

flowering white dogwood, willow,
geranium, basil. I could tell him
chili with black beans, gazpacho,
crusty Italian bread. Maybe he
won't notice he's not there.

Linda Elkin

The Moment for Which There Is No Name

On the sixteenth floor of one of the tall old buildings in the north end of the city, the windows of a vacant apartment look out over the bay. The apartment is empty, the floors and walls bare. There is only a chalked circle on the living room floor. The circle traces the spot where an armchair once stood, an armchair in which an old man regularly sat watching the smokestacks come and go in the harbor in the same way he had watched the swaying forests of masts when he was a boy, years before he became a bookkeeper for one of the city's three tool and die works.

The circle was drawn by the old man's grandson, while the child's parents were supervising the movers.

Tomorrow the new occupants will arrive, and preparatory to moving in they will clean the apartment. In the course of their cleaning, they will erase the chalk.

That is the moment for which there is no name.

Morton Marcus

Letter to Terry Dobson

Here it is June, Maine, overcast.
Where you are I don't know.
Spirit. Ash. River.
Here we think about death sometimes.
Mostly it's darkness.
Mostly a dark cloak of wings.

I remember when your children
and mine were together that time,
all of us . . . eating, drinking,
telling stories. Just walking
from the house to the car
you had to stop to breathe.
Even then the breath was going
out of the body. Even then
your shadow on the grass
was filling itself.

Of course we all want to know
what death is like. Is it bits of fur,
skin, claws, by an old log? Is it
a great mouth that swallows you down
with brine and darkness? Is it a light
out there somewhere? Or is it just
lights out and the distant movement
of slow beings towards this flesh?
We don't wait long for answers.
You know the way it is: all
those lists and then lying down.

Today I miss you, you
and your big belly, the wake-the-dead snore,
your heart like a tea-cup.
You weren't here long enough.
Tell me, what do tears mean there?
What does hair mean? What
does breath mean? Shadow?
Sunlight? Beehive?

Abbot Cutler

Obituaries

I go to them first
even before headlines,
scanning for names I know

even obscurely: fathers of faint
boyhood friends who drove
us twice to a matinee in sleet.

What I seek to apply
is the prefix *trans*:

transport, transbay,
from this quilted chair
on earth, to wherever go
the deceased,

    and to steep in the queer
bridging knowledge

of knowing flesh

which went and leapt the realm.

Eric Zuckerman

The Black and the Dazzle

Some winter mornings
dawn a wild, dazzling bright
finding and blessing everything—
fence post, phone pole
brown grasses poking through snow,
brown cattail medley at the frozen marsh—
with its particular self.
The cold air holds nothing
but transparent possibility.
My daughter
beside me on the seat
chatters along of what she remembers
of summer, the races we had
in the yard on her birthday.
We pass a snowplow, coming at us
and find ourselves for a panicked second
with nothing but each other.
My father writes:
"I am deteriorating steadily and painlessly."
Again the road appears, with
mailboxes, pollarded trees around a farmhouse
and a black line of cattle
strung feeding along a line of hay.

Tom Rea

Valencia Street

You find yourself on a street you've never
walked, in the town you grew up in
and came back to. The street is a ribbon
on a gift you've never opened. You walk the street
and a waft of jasmine fills you, a white cat
crosses your path, and from an open window
you hear the sound of a violin. Garlic
is in the air, and you think of the dish
in your favorite restaurant that you've wanted to try
but end up ordering the spaghetti.
You go to the restaurant and take a seat
on the other side of the room, by the window,
and order *Faraona arrosto al limone.* It's *wonderful!*
Now you know you're on to something.
You stroll to your favorite bookstore and find
the poet you keep hearing about
but haven't read. You buy the book.
You're a blind man finding Braille. She leads you
through streets you've never walked, feeds you words
that taste fresh, full of garlic. You
find yourself. All of a sudden you've bungee jumped
into a new life, you want to free fall
with nothing holding you back. You're ready to walk
that mountain loop you'd always thought too long.
You're free of something you didn't know
had a hold of you, like a ghost
you've lived with and just found, the haunting over.

Robert Funge

Wilderness Poem

I walk, trails stop.
I stop, the compass spins.

Head, shoulders, fins
etched in rain-washed stone.

The body a petroglyph, brittle air
sunlight and blood.

The universe a fragile empire
dissolved on the tongue.

I follow deer tracks beyond clouds.
Lost again,

where the world begins.

John Brandi

Dreaming Them Into the World Again

I'm dreaming him into the world again,
how we're walking together down by the spring
and he looks tall as a tree beside me.

Now I'm a tree and he's the ground,
no, I am myself and him and her, all of us
moving together here in the woods

lost and found together
holding my children and children of my children
in bright suspension like falling leaves.

So where are we going?
Now we can go anywhere.
I can carry us all in my gigantic arms.

We hurry on from place to place
touching each one with our lips
so that green shoots sprout.

I am larger than the earth, two steps
and I've circled the globe.
Everywhere, every place, there are trees!

Tina Letcher

what have you lost and found?

Notes on the Contributors

Michael Nye (cover photographs) grew up in Corpus Christi, Texas. He practiced law for seven years before turning to photography full time in 1984. He has lectured and shown his work internationally, in places including Saudi Arabia, Finland, Morocco, India, and Mexico. "I like to think of portraiture as a way to engage in conversation and a way to listen. The portrait for me continues to be haunting. I always think of a quote I heard—*'what is forgotten is lost.'* Almost every portrait I have made, this quote is somewhere nearby. The person I met, talked to, and photographed becomes just a shadow of that person on photographic paper. There is always so much more to know."

* * *

Tom Absher (page 73) grew up in Texas but now lives and teaches in rural Vermont. "As a teenager, I experienced one of the paradoxes of loss, namely that in order to discover myself as an artist and poet, I had to let go of my unfeeling, macho, controlling images and ideas of who I thought I was. When I *lost* who I was trying to be, I *gained* who I really was. This process began in my teenage years and I have continued to struggle with it ever since!"

Ali Abunimah (page 149) grew up in London and Belgium and now works at the Chapin Hall Center for Children in Chicago, Illinois. "While I was growing up, I learned from my parents that we had lost our homeland of Palestine, where they were born. This enormous loss was revealed to us children through small words and experiences, until we came to understand what grief is. But our memories and determination are harder than earth and stones, which is why we still have never lost hope."

Teresa Palomo Acosta (page 109) grew up in McGregor, Texas, with her maternal grandfather, Maximino Palomo, at her side. "He introduced me to literature through his own stories—*cuentos*—about his life as a cowboy and actor in Mexican folk dramas. Whenever he left town to spend time with my uncle's family in the Panhandle of Texas, I felt his loss tremendously. I was left with no *cuentos* to hear. I had to keep them close to me through my memory. Years later, I still long for his stories and have perhaps become a writer to remember gifts and losses, always trying to keep alive my people's history and forge some of my own . . ."

Amy Adams (page 10) grew up in northern Indiana and now lives with her husband in Austin, Texas. "A few years ago I had this wonderful experience of being nanny to six remarkable friends, one of whom is the subject of 'Nine.' He reminded me so much of myself at that age: anxious, lonely, desperate to have someone nearby. He seemed lost in the crowd of children, and I tried my best to help him find himself. I thought maybe I could save him from the doom he saw in every corner. My time with him was just under a year. After I had left his life, I drove by his house and saw him in the window upstairs staring into the dark night. This poem is my way of coping with that loss. It is my way of saying *Good-bye, friend. I haven't forgotten you either.*"

Lavonne J. Adams (page 38) grew up in Norfolk, Virginia, and now teaches at the University of North Carolina–Wilmington. "Like countless other teenagers, I was a teenager when my parents divorced, and my mother remarried that same year, making me feel as if I had been jettisoned rather abruptly into an adult world. Nothing was constant—not even the colors of crayons."

Linda Allardt (page 57) grew up in small towns in northern Ohio near Lake Erie and in New York State, "both places lost to me now except in memory, but that, of course, is the wellspring of my writing." Once her friend referred to in "Written for You" was gone, "I found myself seeing so much more I wanted to tell him, and did, the only way I could, in poems . . ."

Maggie Anderson (page 59) was born in New York City and has moved twenty times in her life. She now lives and teaches in Ohio. "When I was nine years old, my mother died of leukemia after a long illness. This was my first, largest, and still most significant loss, the filter through which I see all others. . . . Every loss has opened up an empty space into which . . . something new has been set to grow."

Brian Andreas (page 96) lives with his wife and two young sons in a big old house in Iowa, "where they make soup and art and stories as often as they can."

Anzai Hitoshi (page 18) was born in Japan in 1919 and worked as a journalist for various newspapers, as well as writing poems and prose about poetry. He died in 1994.

Philip Appleman (page 47) directed the creative writing program at Indiana University for many years and now lives on the eastern end of Long Island. He has published numerous books of poetry, fiction, and nonfiction. "Growing up during the Great Depression was a more or less constant experience of loss: loss of jobs, loss of hope—and then, during World War II, the tragic loss . . . of many friends and relatives. No doubt those memories helped inspire the poem included here. . . . [T]here was also in those days a tenacious spirit that somehow got people through . . . with renewed hope of making a better world for the next generation."

Nuala Archer (page 110) has lived in Ireland and Cleveland and presently lives in Jerusalem—writing, painting, and working with a theater/visual arts group. "I'm a clinger, but when I lose my grip, when I let go my hold, then I see things alive & whole (after, of course, the first few moments of terror & loss of consciousness). Then I can breathe again. To lose or be lost quickens everything. Then I am so close to zen that my soul feels reconnected to its source."

173

Jimmy Santiago Baca (page 72) is a widely travelled, best-selling poet from New Mexico.

Jan Bailey (page 21) lives and conducts poetry workshops on Monhegan Island, Maine. She is the author of *Paper Clothes*, and her poems have appeared in many magazines.

Richard Beban (page 114) moderates workshops, writes screenplays, and runs a poetry reading series in Venice, California. "As a teenager I hated anything that reeked of losing and a 'loser' was someone confined to the lowest level of teenage Hell. But . . . I've learned since that life is loss and we eventually measure ourselves by how we learn from it. . . . Find your own voice, your own guiding spirit, what the Greeks called your *daimon*, or genius, and you will be able to incorporate loss as the gift it can be. . . ."

Bruce Bennett (page 65) teaches at Wells College in Aurora, New York. As he gets older, he finds he has more and more to say, though he's not sure he's saying it better. But he still likes his poem.

Vittorio Bodini (page 24) was born in Bari, Italy, in 1914 and died in Rome in 1970. He published five books of poems and worked as a professor and translator.

Catherine Bowman (page 144) was born in El Paso, Texas. She graduated from high school and college in San Antonio, and currently lives in Bloomington, where she teaches creative writing at Indiana University. "What did I lose as a teenager? So many things. My favorite gold filigree earrings that my grandmother gave to me, my red ten-speed (it was stolen), a hand-painted antique rose tea-cup (it broke), keys, money, homework, my cat Cosmos, and a book of poems by Nikki Giovanni that I had stolen from the library."

Lisa Brandenburg (page 36) teaches at St. Mark's School of Texas in Dallas. "Someone said all creative urges are part of a longing to get back to the place we all came from, a place where we all existed as divine creative forces. What have we lost? That's what we're here to work on."

John Brandi (page 169) lives along the Rio Grande in New Mexico. Painter as well as poet and essayist, his books include *Heartbeat Geography* and *Weeding the Cosmos: Selected Haiku*.

Jack Brannon (page 142) lives in Austin, Texas, where he explores the creeks with his Labrador retriever, Abby. "It was hard for me as I began to learn that many things in my life would not be forever. My father developed a heart problem and I was gripped by fear of losing him. He was my best friend. My grandparents died and their home and farm were sold. We lost our family's 'home base.' That was a loss of place and self that I felt then and still feel."

Henry Braun (page i) lives and dreams in the Maine woods. Sometimes he finds his lost teenage years in poems. When he was fifteen, a teacher told him that he wasn't "running on all cylinders." One cylinder had its eye closed for dreaming.

Jay Bremyer (page 146) lives on the Kansas prairie with his wife, Sara. "Often, upon awakening, I reach back toward the rich, fluid world of dreams, but it slips away. Going to sleep, I lose contact with the daytime world. Some difficult moments I prefer to lose, at least temporarily, by moving from one world into the other. But ultimately I think we're here to create good stories from all that we experience."

Kimberly J. Brown (page 49) was born in Korea and adopted as a baby by an American family. She graduated from the University of Minnesota in 1998. "Poetry is like a giant cabin I have all to myself. I can go there every day to visit. I can throw down my belongings in a heap, kick, crumple, rearrange, fold, put away, or wash. . . . [T]he way we respond to loss is part of what makes us most human, most strong, most fragile. . . . Poetry is a place . . . for telling the truth: where loss can roam around and fill our senses . . . where our terror and joy at the aliveness of ourselves and everyone around us can be reborn."

Rosellen Brown (page 84) is a best-selling novelist and poet, currently living in Chicago.

Jenny Browne (page 78) grew up on a humid, muddy bend of the Ohio River in Evansville, Indiana. She now teaches and writes in San Antonio, Texas. "I lose phone numbers, running shoes, bills, and especially parked cars. Unlike organized people, when I lose something, it can be hiding absolutely anywhere. . . . I often find other things, pictures, half-written letters . . . that overshadow what I lost in the first place. . . . Lately I've become interested in the space that opens up when someone important leaves. . . . I'm amazed at what I find there, even if it is only a quiet emptiness."

Ernesto Cardenal (page 82) was born in Nicaragua in 1925. He has said of his own work, "I tried principally to write poetry that can be understood."

Héctor Carreto (page 102) lives and writes in Mexico.

Cyrus Cassells (page 128) has worked as a translator, film critic, actor, and professor. He lived in Italy for many years and has recently moved to Wimberley, Texas.

Fran Castan (page 134) teaches writing and literature every spring at the School of Visual Arts in New York, New York, her native city. Her first husband, a correspondent for *Look* magazine, covered the war in Vietnam until he was killed there. "When I was a teenager . . . my good friend and I would wonder about death. We couldn't understand it. We still can't. How does a person—such a unique, precious complexity—leave us? We know where the body is, but where is *she*? Where is *he*? Even with answers from science and religion, the death of each of us remains our greatest mystery."

Siv Cedering (page 14) was born near the Arctic Circle in Sweden and moved to San Francisco, California, when she was fourteen. She now lives near the ocean in Amagansett, New York. Painter and sculptor as well as author of eighteen books, she has written half of them in Swedish, including a series for children about a pig.

Hayan Charara (page 91) grew up Arab in Detroit. He writes, "I learned how to recite the Fatihah, the opening prayer of the Quran, before I memorized the words to the 'Star-Spangled Banner.'" Currently he lives in New York.

Eric Chock (page 130) writes, "'Tutu on the Curb' is the kind of free association that comes with living in Honolulu for a lifetime. Seeing an old woman getting off a bus reminded me of old women I saw in the same neighborhood when I was young. Something in the way they dressed up in their *mu'u mu'u* to go *holoholo* downtown was touching to me, and the poem evolved out of a simple desire to capture the image, one that is too rapidly disappearing from our scene."

Martha Christina (page 8) grew up in Indiana and now lives in Rhode Island, where she teaches creative writing at Roger Williams University. ". . . as a teenager, my thoughts were all centered on winning: winning friends, sports competitions, beauty contests, offices in clubs, etc., and I found every loss (of course, there were many) a heartbreaking surprise. At the time, I thought I would never get over each individual loss, and was equally surprised when I did. All along I was learning about the resiliency of the human spirit, but I couldn't have said so then."

Lucille Clifton (pages 66, 89) is one of America's best-loved poets. She has taught widely, received many awards, and currently lives in Maryland.

Joan Colby (page 150) lives on a small horse farm in northern Illinois. "What does one lose as one grows older? Energy, certainty, ambition. What does one gain? Wisdom, I hope. And a kind of acceptance one can't imagine, nor shouldn't, as a young person."

Brittney Corrigan (page 30) grew up in Colorado and now lives in Oregon, where she graduated from Reed College. "As a teenager, I lost my grandfather, which, when coupled with my parents' divorce, awakened the need in me to record the stories of my family, the histories and landscapes of our lives."

Abbot Cutler (page 164) grew up outside Boston and now lives in western Massachusetts with his wife and their sons. "The loss that hurts, no matter what age, is the loss of friend or family."

Craig Czury (page 77) lives in Pennsylvania. He writes, "Opposite of what I was told, you can go home and you can take home with you, only don't expect the mother any clearer or the father in their silence. The lies were simple jokes, I heard them my whole life. And now, on the way to religion I go home, pronounce all the unpronounceable names in the obituary. I play your voice through my cello."

Robert Dana (page 1) lives in Iowa. His most recent book is *Hello, Stranger*. "Orphaned at the age of eight by the death of my mother and desertion by my father, I knew far too much about loss. Mine was the kind you never really get over."

Phebe Davidson (page 87) teaches English at the University of South Carolina–Aiken. "I grew up in my grandmother's house, where my parents and I came to live when my mother had the first of many breakdowns. By the time I was a teenager, my mother was a heavy drinker and tranquilizer user who still had breakdowns. My father was a full-time factory worker and weekend musician. Even though they were tangible presences in my life, I felt that I had lost my parents and cherished a formless hope that I would find them somewhere and we would be okay. Mine wasn't a terrible adolescence, but in this regard it was very wistful."

Diana Der-Hovanessian (page 160) lives and writes in Cambridge, Massachusetts. She is the foremost translator of Armenian poetry into English.

Camille Domangue (page 131) of San Antonio, Texas, was dying of cancer at age forty-three as this book was being compiled. She said, "Just say I lost everything."

Linda Elkin (page 162) lives in San Francisco, California, and teaches writing. "As a teenager, whenever I suffered a loss of any kind, I was very secretive about it. One of the pleasures of growing up was finding people with whom I could share my thoughts and feelings."

William I. Elliott (page 6) grew up in Chicago, Illinois. Fifteen years later he grew up a second time in graduate school, and then began growing up again in Japan, where he has lived and taught for twenty-five years. He is still growing up. "I never lost myself until I began finding myself. I am lucky to be able to say Lost and Found rather than Found and Lost. Finder's keepers."

Nick Flynn (page 52) lives in Brooklyn, New York, and works for the Writing Project at Columbia University's Teachers College. "The summer before my mother killed herself, I had been living on a boat. . . . [T]he next summer I began, with a friend, to rebuild another boat, ruined and enormous . . . built in 1939, the same year my mother was born. . . . Eventually it did float again and we anchored it a quarter mile offshore from Provincetown. . . . I was strangely comforted by the knowledge that I could go to sleep any night and wake up the next morning with land nowhere in sight . . . the tide having pulled me far out to sea. This everpresent possibility of finding myself suddenly lost in deep water mirrored the sense of loss I felt at my mother's death, how quickly one's life could be altered . . ."

Ken Fontenot (page 45) was born in New Orleans and now lives in Austin, Texas, where he works as a technical writer for a computer company.

Zymunt Frankel (page 147) lives in Israel. One of his chapbooks is called *Slightly Nasty Poems*.

Dwight Fullingim (page 101) was born a sixth-generation Texan and now lives and works in Saudi Arabia. His recent book is *Glory Land*. "I grew up in a series of Baptist parsonages in small Texas towns . . . endured the loss of friends and connections many times due to moves. . . . Lost faith in the abiding integrity of American political motives during the Vietnam War era. Lost respect for the Baptist faith as practiced by ignorant, racist preachers and congregations, but retained liking for the music and covered-dish dinners. . . ."

Robert Funge (page 168) is a native of San Francisco, California, and now lives down the peninsula in San Carlos. "The loss I didn't feel as a teenager was felt later and is one of the sources of my poetry and a springboard for life. As Octavio Paz said, "Loss [is] the first step toward fullness."

Jack Gilbert (page 88) writes, "I am living on a bare mountain in Greece (on the island of Paros) listening to the clatter of goat bells. I think about the largeness and difficulties and riches of *serious* romantic love. (Not the fun part.) And try to find my poems."

Ángel González (page 25), originally from Spain, has said, "My long stay in America has not helped to integrate me here; on the other hand, its effect was to distance me from Spain, which during my absence became in fact another country, much better and more livable than the one I remember as mine. . . ." (*Paintbrush* interview, 1991)

Linda Gregg (page 35) was born in California and has also lived in Greece and Massachusetts. She writes, "This poem is about the feeling of loss when we leave home permanently. And the strange feeling of being alone physically and emotionally."

James Baker Hall (page 53) lives in rural Kentucky. He is a poet, photographer, professor, and basketball fan.

Joy Harjo (page 138) of the Mvskoke Nation is an award-winning poet and saxophone player. Author of many collections, she also has a CD, *Letter from the End of the Twentieth Century*, with her band, Joy Harjo and Poetic Justice. "I was being introduced a few years ago in Texas. . . . The audience was packed. . . . The introducer, extremely well-prepared . . . brought up places I had been, accomplishments from the distant past that I had forgotten. It was almost embarrassing. . . . I told [the audience] they should have seen a list of all my failures, my losses, for that list would have been ten times as long, even a hundred times as long . . . including loss of self-respect before I was five years old because I was beaten by my father, or becoming pregnant at sixteen . . . and losing many years raising two children without fathers, money, or support. I lost my childhood. What I have learned, though, is the universe is huge and carries the memory of everything that ever happened, every lost thing. Poems often carry these memories. And sometimes when I think I have lost something, I eventually find it, in another shape and size, at another time."

Carla Hartsfield (page 92) was born in Waxahachie, Texas, and immigrated to Canada in 1982. "Because I began piano study at the age of four, my childhood and teen years were filled with the discipline of practicing and . . . the seemingly endless preparation for concerts and competitions. I grew up with a sense that my psychological and emotional welfare was tied to the piano alone. When I seriously began to write poetry in my mid-twenties, all of that changed. It was my lifeline . . . back to my authentic self, which at that point in time I was convinced I'd lost. . . . The person in 'Shrink-wrapped' is a composite of individuals I've known who have failed to grab the wonderful opportunities that come along."

David Hassler (page 7) lives and works as a poet-in-the-schools in Ohio. He and his wife edited an oral history–photography book about urban gardeners. "I often had the feeling growing up that my father was absent from the house when he was in his study reading or writing. Eventually I discovered my own passion to read and disappear into books—it felt like a secret we shared. I began to understand my father better and to forgive his absence."

Mick Hatten (page 136) was born and educated in Minnesota and currently works as a sportswriter in Iowa. "As a teenager, I was on a VFW baseball team that had reached the state tournament every year of its existence, and we lost in the district final. I replayed that game in my mind over and over. . . . I think I learned a great deal about perseverance, how to pick myself up after the losses I suffered. . . . [T]hose things have stayed with me throughout my life."

Jane Hirshfield (page 153) grew up in New York City and now lives in a small white cottage in northern California, where she grows fruit trees, vegetables, herbs, and flowers in her garden. She is the author of four books of poetry and a book of essays about poetry. She has taught at many universities, and travels widely to read her poems.

Tony Hoagland (page 124) teaches at New Mexico State University in Las Cruces. "I feel a particular sympathy for boys and men and their struggles in growing up. 'The Question,' for me, is about male silence, which is often about not looking foolish or weak."

Harriet Jacobs (page 26) lives and writes in Los Angeles, California. . . . "when we leave, we will take only what we brought to this world, what we learned from it—so what can we ever really lose?"

Rolf Jacobsen (page 90) was born in 1907 and is widely considered to be one of the greatest of Norway's poets of the twentieth century. He died in 1994.

Roger Jones (page 40) teaches at Southwest Texas State University. "I've always had a really heavy awareness of time and time passing. . . . [E]ven as a teenager, I was lamenting the past, feeling quite uncomfortable about the speed with which . . . experiences rush by. . . . I think awareness of time and its passing is the one great theme of lyric poetry."

June Jordan (page 60) has published more than twenty-three books, has taught African American Studies at the University of California, Berkeley, where she also directs the "Poetry for the People" project, and is a widely respected activist for many causes.

Ben Judson's (page 85) poem was written "while flying home to Texas from Oaxaca, Mexico, where I gained my solitude, which is a gain that feels so much like a loss it could be truth itself. Indeed, the Virgin of Solitude is worshipped in Oaxaca more than in any other city. How could I have felt but that I had left behind my newfound loss?"

Kasey Jueds (page 145) grew up in New Jersey and England. "As a teenager, I didn't talk much about loss, but I know that's when I started to wonder about it. . . . [W]here did lost things, dreams, friends, go? Sometimes I think poems are an attempt to find that place, to put my hands on what has vanished."

Vickie Karp (page 83) grew up in New York City, where she has lost, over the years, a gold ring in the shape of two hearts, half of a two-piece bathing suit in a locker room at Rockaway Playland, the only copy of a poem she wrote about Thanksgiving, a parakeet named Beauty who flew out an open window, and more.

David Keefe (page 152) lives in Bristol, England, where he edits Weatherlight Press, publishing contemporary American poetry. "Early one morning in 1996 I was listening to the car radio when someone explained how a shout is sometimes enough to start an avalanche. I immediately stopped the car and wrote 'Ghazal (For William Stafford).' It reminds us that everything we do has an effect. That perhaps we gain more (or lose less) by listening to the world rather than shouting at mountains! A lesson the poems of William Stafford continue to teach me."

Jane Kenyon (page 99) was born in 1947 and died in 1995 of leukemia. She published four collections of poems and was featured with her husband, poet Donald Hall, in the Emmy Award–winning Bill Moyers/David Grubin Special "A Life Together."

Patricia Kirkpatrick (page 94) teaches writing at Hamline University in Saint Paul, Minnesota. Her picture book *Plowie: A Story from the Prairie* honors the grandmother whose death she grieves in her poem here.

Judith Kitchen (page 17) lives in Brockport, New York, on the original Erie Canal. She grew up in the small town of Painted Post, New York, where teenagers often met each other on the ice-skating pond. "But it wasn't until I saw my own son one day, almost a stranger on the ice, that I realized parents must prepare for loss from the day their child is born. . . . I wanted my poem to reflect both points of view— his, as I could only imagine it (having been a teenager myself), and mine, as it was hitting me full force."

Ted Kooser (page 158) lives on an acreage near Garland, Nebraska. He says loss is a part of every poem he's written. "Sometimes it is grieved, sometimes cele- brated, but always there somewhere—"

Lan Se (page 155) is among a group of younger "city poets" in China whose work is described as being direct and ironic. His name is a pseudonym meaning "the color blue."

Sandra Larson (page 42) lives in Minnesota and remembers her teen years as "heady with energy, enthusiasm, angst. Everything had to do with things being too big or too little—nose and thighs too large, breasts too small, hometown too little, the wide world too big. I wondered what it would be like when I lost my virginity and my excuse for daydreaming—when I had to leave school and get a job. As it turns out, loss is just the flip side of gain and gain the flip side of loss."

Donna Lee (page 74) used to teach in the public schools in San Antonio, Texas. If she finds us, we'll send her a copy of this book!

Tina Letcher (page 170) teaches ESL in Rhode Island. "I grew up in the woods of upstate New York, happy exploring by myself or with my dad. When he died, I was just out of my teen years and nobody would talk about it. It has taken many years and dreams for me to learn how to mourn and celebrate him."

Robert Hill Long (page 159) writes, "I was raised on the hurricane coast of North Carolina, and acquainted at an early age with alligators, water moccasins, sting rays, and sharks. Now I live in rainy western Oregon and work with young writers at the University of Oregon. I started writing poems at fifteen (still believ- ing my destiny involved rock-singer stardom) because I lost a bet with a girl I loved named Jane. The bet was about a Duke/UNC basketball game; I had to write Jane five poems. They didn't make her fall in love with me, but in writing them I fell in love with poetry. I still find its words and rhythms the best way to recover all that I've lost in life, in time. . . . And Jane—once my muse—is still my friend, and has a copy of each of my books."

Chris Mahon (page 81) works as an editor for a high-tech information company in the San Francisco (California) Bay Area. He lost innumerable things as a teenager, including a turquoise ring in the Rocky Mountains; the chance to kiss a girl on the Ferris wheel at Elitch's Gardens; and a home-run derby baseball game to his older brother Rick, 38–3.

Nancy Mairs (page 64) won the Western States Book Award for her stunning poetry collection, *In All the Rooms of the Yellow House.*

Morton Marcus (page 163), author of seven books of poetry and one novel, was born in New York City and spent almost his entire youth in boarding schools. "So loss—in this case, loss of family life—was a fact of daily existence." As a teenage athlete, he frustrated his coaches by not caring whether he won or lost . . . "playing the game was where it was at." As an adult, "loss was held at bay . . . by writing experiences and dreams into their own never-ending existence."

Dionisio D. Martínez (page 2) says, "Once you've lost a country—I was born in Cuba, in 1956—there isn't much left to lose. You learn to move on, holding on to what remains: you mold what you can and adapt to the rest. It helps to have parents and a few real friends who support your unconventional search. Over the years, I've discovered Sinatra, Mingus, Eliot, Cortazar, O'Keeffe, Kierkegaard. . . . [S]o far, my discoveries outnumber my losses. It's been a sweet ride and I look forward to much more."

Marissa C. Martínez (page 100), originally from San Antonio, Texas, now makes her home in Seattle, where she earns her living as a software engineer. She is completing work on a poetry manuscript based on the oral histories of her family. "I have often wondered what happens in the lives of what is lost to us—the interesting story is in the continuing."

Barbara McCauley (page 4) lives in Truchas, New Mexico, where she practices losing herself moment by moment through zazen, writing, painting, cooking, gardening, gazing, and dreaming.

Susie Mee (page 5) lives in New York City and teaches at New York University. "As the daughter of an undertaker and someone who was obsessed . . . with death, my growing up years were filled with loss. I'm writing a book about this now."

Bill Meissner (page 16) grew up in Iowa and Wisconsin and now teaches at St. Cloud State University in Minnesota. "The lack of communication between a parent and a child is one of the most poignant losses we can experience. It's important to cultivate communication with each other before that irreversible loss—death—makes it too late."

Emma Mellon (page 23) is a psychologist and writer living in the Philadelphia, Pennsylvania, suburbs. "As a pre-teen, I wrote mystery stories and poetry, but as a teenager, I lost touch with the writer in me. Happily, menopause has brought her back. It's great to be together again!"

Susan V. Meyers (page 154) lives in Seattle, Washington, and writes, "As a young woman recovering from my parents' recent divorce, I've learned that the experience of loss is not about absence so much as it is about growth. Loss is not an issue of departed things or people; instead, it is concerned with what remains: my self."

Pat Mora (page 19) writes, "My four grandparents came to El Paso, Texas, at the time of the Mexican Revolution. I was born in that border city, as were my three children. I remember them as teenagers, I remember the teens I taught, and I remember myself as a teenager. I remember many of my feelings then, but I didn't save anything I wrote. I wish I had."

Haas H. Mroue (page 68) was born in Beirut, Lebanon, and now lives in San Diego, California. He is co-author of a new Frommer's Europe guide. "I entered my teenage years having lost many things—the home I grew up in, the friends I grew up with, even the simple pleasure of biking on sunny mornings in the hills near my grandparents' house. War changed everything overnight, imposing a loss so sudden and so huge that even now as an adult, whenever I experience a loss, I regress back to a state of helplessness and to those first days of war when everything I knew was reduced to one giant swirl of dust behind our speeding car."

Harryette Mullen (page 28) teaches African American literature and creative writing at the University of California, Los Angeles. "While my poem 'Shedding Skin' is more about renewal and transformation than loss, I know about the other side of losing. You might say I've always been a loser. . . . I've had a tendency to let go of things: mittens, hats, socks, my Mickey Mouse watch—once even a favorite broken-in pair of shoes that were sucked into a whirlpool as I was crossing a creek. My mother told me many times that if I paid more attention to what I was doing, my possessions would not be so eager to leave me. . . . Sometimes I think our small losses might be little rehearsals for the terrible losses that threaten to undo us. Maybe they teach us something useful about ourselves and how we recover from the ache of losing something we care about. . . ."

Jack Myers (page 58), born in Massachusetts, directs the creative writing program at Southern Methodist University in Dallas, Texas. "'Leaving the Light On' is a teenager's naive attempt to objectively see his parents for who they really were. It was part of what I felt I had lost as a teenager . . . the power-base of a unified sense of self that early on lends one dignity and confidence. . . . [C]racking open the door of manhood and announcing myself to the world, everything I thought I knew, including myself, got sucked out into the . . . zero-gravity of the void. Thus began my life as a poet."

Jim Natal (page xiv) grew up on the south side of Chicago, Illinois, and now lives in Los Angeles, California, where he works as executive editor for the National Football League Properties. A collector of Zuñi fetish carvings, he favors mountain lions. "I was very lucky as a teenager that most of my experiences of loss were from dealing with the deaths of pets, rejection by girls, and playing on a high school football team that never won a game. Most of the material things I have lost I don't miss. I believe almost anything lost can be replaced, except for love, loved ones, time, and an opportunity to say nothing."

Leonard Nathan (page 46) has lived most of his adult life in northern California, but his childhood was spent in southern California, where he began writing poetry, "which was (and I think, still is) a compensation for what had been denied me or I had lost, though I could not have explained *what* I had lost; I just knew that on certain days a vast absence hung over a landscape of which I was merely one solitary part."

Denise Overfield (page 44) once lived in Pittsburgh, Pennsylvania, as part of the Carlow College community. We can't find her now. Please, Denise, find us!

Charles Owsley (page 106) works in sports medicine at a high school in San Antonio, Texas. "Like the trains, I too left my small hometown for the city and its promise of better things. Even now, the whistle reminds me of the wonder and excitement I thought would be waiting here."

Heberto Padilla (page 29) is considered one of Cuba's foremost poets, now living in exile in the United States. His memoir is *Self-Portrait of the Other*.

Nicanor Parra (page 129) is a Chilean poet, born in 1914, well known for writing "anti-poems," which emphasize the absurdity of daily life.

Chris Pealer (page 20) grew up in Ohio and now teaches in a private high school in Dallas, Texas. "At age fourteen, I started writing with a group of friends . . . passing around a folder (soon several) of various scribblings, some funny, some unspeakably bizarre. This continued throughout high school. . . . Everyone suffers some kind of loss. It is the source of our compassion for one another. I wish I had more control over it. At times it seems I careen through the world, losing track of money and days and people. . . . I wake up later humbled and shocked. Yet I believe things will come to fill the spaces. Hopefully, good things. . . . Did I mention we lost the folders too? They disappeared behind a misty curtain. They no doubt reside in Camelot, atop a dragon's pile of gold."

Robert Phillips (page 126) grew up on the eastern shore of Delaware, where what was most lost to him was anything related to culture. He fled to New York State at age eighteen and never returned. Currently he is Moores University Scholar at the University of Houston.

David B. Prather (page 156) was born and raised in West Virginia, where he now teaches English and creative writing and is an MFA candidate at Warren Wilson College. "The poem 'Avalanche' is a scenic attempt to recall, from young adulthood, the loss of my paternal grandfather, as well as create a paternal grandmother—a woman who died before I was born."

Quintin Prout (page 97) was born and raised in Providence, Rhode Island, where he now edits *The Spoken Jazz Press*. "As a teenager, I was devastated by the death of my older brother, and even though family and friends pulled together in support of one another, what truly saved me back then was the ability to write my feelings down on paper. It's something that continues to save me to this day."

Leroy V. Quintana (page 148) is a native New Mexican currently teaching in San Diego, California. His new book is *The Great Whirl of Exile*.

Tom Rea (page 167) lives in Casper, Wyoming, where he worked for many years for a newspaper and now is writing a book about dinosaurs, people, and the science that connects them. He is the parent of an eight-year-old and two teenagers, who go through fascinating cycles of losing themselves and then finding themselves again.

Alastair Reid (page 62) was born in Scotland in 1926 and has lived since 1984 primarily in the Dominican Republic, on a remote peninsula. He has been on the staff of the *New Yorker* and has published dozens of marvelous books.

Frances Richard (page 161) lives and teaches in Brooklyn, New York. "I am part of the fourth generation of my family to live in our house, and ghosts are part of the familiar material . . . the space between dishes and canned goods on the shelves. When my grandfather died, I knew he had simply slipped 'cross the air into that part of the house where other family members who had gone before were waiting for him, and the things he left behind had a little shine to them now, because he left them with us. . . . I have learned on a fundamental level that invisible does not mean disappeared."

Jack Ridl (page 48) teaches English at Hope College in Holland, Michigan. He grew up in Pittsburgh. "I was a pretty good athlete, but more interested in what it was like to be a part of sports. . . . [T]he combinations of grace, improvisation, impact, discipline, technique, and vision I learned playing ball have, I hope, carried over into the poetry. The irony is my father [famous basketball coach Buzz Ridl] was a winning coach—my poems, like most poems, concern themselves with loss."

Geoff Rips (page 120) has been publisher of *The Texas Observer* in Austin, is father of two significant daughters, and currently is a fellow of the Open Society Institute of the Soros Foundation. "What we lose remains in this universe, but over time it falls farther and farther away from the known, moving toward the unknown."

Renato Rosaldo (page 32) is a widely published cultural anthropologist at Stanford University, whose current research concerns cultural citizenship and racial democracy.

Vern Rutsala (page 70) was born on a farm in Idaho but has spent most of his adult years in Oregon. "One of the worst losses I remember from high school days was a very literal one—I quarterbacked our team to a 57–7 loss. My dreams of a Heisman Trophy ended there, but I kept writing, thinking I might last longer that way though it entails a few losses here and there."

John Sangster (page 86) lives and writes happily on an island off the coast of Washington.

John Phillip Santos (page 141) lost his Moroccan silver bracelet, with filigreed obsidian inlay, in Kenya. He left the journal of his journey to the Sudan in a New York City cab.

Susan Marie Scavo (page 140) spent her growing-up years in Cincinnati, Ohio, and now lives in rural Vermont. Like everyone, she has lost many things, but believes there is one thing that can't be lost. The thing that makes us who we are. The one thing that is different for each of us.

Peter Sears (page 61) works for *Rubberstampmadness*, the rubber-stamping magazine in Corvallis, Oregon. He admits, reluctantly, that "he suffered no major loss in his childhood. But losing, that's another matter."

Alison Seevak (page 118) lives in Albany, California, with her two cats and Sophie, a golden retriever.

Sekine Hiroshi (page 112) was born in Tokyo in 1920 and began working to earn a living at the age of twelve. He became active in left-wing democratic movements, writing social and literary criticism, novels, plays, and poetry. He died in 1994.

Reza Shirazi (page 67), Iranian by origin, was born and raised in Bombay, India. "My first language as a toddler was Persian, but when I went to an English school, English replaced it. . . . I had a Persian tutor . . . but stopped . . . when I was in my early teens. When I went to graduate school at the University of Texas, I took Persian classes to brush up my ability to read and write, which I had almost forgotten. My wish is to someday read Rumi's poems in the original Persian."

Jeffrey Shotts (page 108) lives in Minnesota and works for Graywolf Press. "I think many young people's first experience with significant loss is through the death of an older relative. . . . Losses are often hidden from young people by their parents until it's time to wade through the detritus . . . very much the case with my experiences growing up in Kansas. The poem is for my mother."

Lisa Ruth Shulman (page 3) lives in New York City and works for a magazine publisher. "As a teenager, I retreated into my room to write poetry in an attempt to understand the irreconcilable conflict of love, loss, and longing. This poem is my memory of a time when I was certain that if I stole upon my father in an unguarded moment, I could catch a glimpse of his affection."

Kirsti Simonsuuri (page 76) was born in Helsinki, Finland, in 1945 and has studied and lived in England, France, West Germany, and the United States.

Hal Sirowitz (page 12) lives in Flushing, New York, where he teaches special education at an elementary school. "When I was a teenager, I thought I was losing out on having a girlfriend, but when I got older, I finally found one. I wasn't a teenager anymore. But it didn't matter. Neither was she."

Margo Solod (page 105) recently moved from a tiny island off the Maine coast to seventy-two acres in the Shenandoah Valley of Virginia, where she is building a log cabin in the saddle between two mountains. She cooks for a living. Although she has lost much in her life, at this point she feels she is "running slightly ahead of the game."

Cathy Song (page 98) lives in Hawai'i. "My father one day made a remark that left me feeling as though I had overheard him speaking to himself . . . some sadness I understood in his voice. He had entered a time . . . when many of his childhood friends were dying, and his turn in this natural progression of birth and death he knew would soon arrive. Sometimes I think losing a friend through misunderstanding can be just as painful. . . . Will your secrets—revealed in the comfort of the friendship—make you vulnerable now that trust is gone? . . . You want to bury the dead, but you can't let go—some part of yourself has been exposed, torn, scattered in places unknown."

Nathan Spoon (page 69) lives and writes in White House, Tennessee. He publishes chapbooks under the Hie Thee Home imprint. He has written, "I will tell you something: life and death are not two things. Or, if they are, they are dancing together—forever."

William Stafford (page 132), one of the most beloved poets of the twentieth century, was born in Kansas in 1914 and died in Oregon in 1993.

Melissa A. Stephenson (page 56) lives in Ithaca, New York, where she works for Literacy Volunteers of America. "What Grandma Taught Her" suggests a way to move through loss, which is what much of her writing is about. As a child, she never spoke of her mother's death. Now, her grief, compassion, and longing have found a voice in her poetry.

Emma Suárez-Báez (page 34) left Puerto Rico at seventeen to pursue a career as a professional dancer. This had "a permanent price—the loss of cultural, territorial, linguistic, and relational continuity"—themes now central in her writing. She is deeply involved with the Writing Project at Columbia University's Teachers College. Married to a police officer, she has two boys, Julian and Andrew, whom she wishes she had named Andreas.

Sandra Gail Teichmann (page 13) grew up in Colorado and now teaches in Canyon, Texas. "Perhaps my greatest loss on becoming a teenager was the passing of timeless days. Never again were the hours endless for the bloom of spirea at the pump house, for sifting sand in a sun-warm sandbox, for Mother peeling peaches for her sterile canning jars, for the wood fires and feather comforters against the cold."

Ernesto Trejo (page 80) taught creative writing at Fresno City College. Edward Hirsch wrote of his work, "Trejo is a poet of mysteries . . . of secret unnamed presences, of the magical interior spaces of childhood and the luminous floating world that flares and throbs, that burns in time."

William Trowbridge (page 37) was born in Chicago, Illinois, and grew up in Omaha, Nebraska, where, as a teenager, had he been taller, better looking, and charismatic, he would have been just like James Dean. But he was more like Buster Keaton, something he learned to enjoy, sort of.

James Tolan (page 43) is from Chicago, Illinois, and now lives on Staten Island, New York. "As a child I had a large Irish and Italian family, many of whom died around the same time. My life changed dramatically—no more weekends at the grandparents' with a big extended family. . . . [P]oetry and stories keep my grandparents and great-grandparents, uncles and aunts alive in my life like breath from their spirits. I miss them all."

Memye Curtis Tucker (page 116) lives in Georgia and is author of *The Watchers*. "My grandmother's father died when she was twelve. . . . [T]hat loss was so great that decades later when I was a teen it was still reverberating through our family. . . . [F]or generations in large and small ways we were affected by the long-ago loss of home and security and the eloquent man whose letters I have just found in a chest, carefully wrapped in linen."

John Vernon (page 104) writes, "'The present is now.' But of course by the time you've finished saying that, *is* has become *was*. Loss is so built into time's flood that sometimes it seems the most remarkable of miracles to wake up in the same room, on the same bed, beside the same person."

Mary Ann Wehler (page 133) lives in Michigan. After thirty-one years of teaching six-year-olds, she has switched to teaching creative writing in libraries, YMCAs, and bookstores.

Jennifer Weinblatt (page 54) was born and raised in New York City. She currently lives with her husband and daughter in Nashville, Tennessee, where she writes and teaches. "I think I experienced my first serious losses in life when I was a teenager: I lost the uncomplicated relationship I had once had with my mother, and the uncomplicated relationship I had once had with my body. . . . Teenagers are often accused of melodrama, but there is a lot of genuine drama inherent in the teenage years, and much of it seems related to all the loss involved in leaving behind a part of your child-self to begin to construct an adult-self."

David Williams (page 33) lives in Worcester, Massachusetts. "When I was in high school, the Vietnam War confronted us with huge questions. How do you respond to the destruction of so many lives? Classmates wounded or killed? People you'd grown up with rejecting you for your beliefs? . . . I lost one sense of belonging and slowly discovered another. The Gulf War opened new and old wounds. At the time, I was doing resettlement work with Indo-Chinese refugees. . . . Our common language half-formed, we talked about Buddha, history, loss, home remedies for sleeplessness, and faith."

Steve Wilson (page 117) lives in San Marcos, Texas, and teaches at Southwest Texas State University. A frequent traveler, he has lived and worked in Malaysia, England, Ireland, and Romania. "In the fall of 1997, the friend to whom 'Part' is dedicated committed suicide. . . . [W]riting about it, and letting my mind reveal to me just how I felt about Tibi's death, [was] a way to come to terms with that loss."

Yamanoguchi Baku (page 113) was born in Okinawa in 1903 and survived the devastating Tokyo earthquake in 1923. He worked various odd jobs in both places and wrote poetry throughout his life. He died in 1963.

Andy Young (page 122) grew up in West Virginia, "where the mountains were riddled with loss." Currently she lives in the French Quarter of New Orleans, Louisiana.

Daisy Zamora (page 22) lives in Nicaragua and is a painter, psychologist, activist for women's issues, and teacher, as well as a poet and mom. She has also been a combatant for the National Sandinista Liberation Front and the Vice-Minister of Culture.

Eric Zuckerman (page 166) studied poetry in Montana and worked as a chef. Currently he is a Jesuit priest in the Oregon Province.

what
have
you lost?

what
have
you lost?

what
have
you found?

Acknowledgments

Naomi Shihab Nye thanks the John Simon Guggenheim Memorial Foundation for their encouraging support and the friends who helped her locate poets, especially Jeffrey Shotts, Bruce Snider, and Daria Donnelly. She especially thanks the amazing Greenwillow team—Phyllis Larkin, Ava Weiss, and Virginia Duncan—for not losing their minds in the midst of so many details.

Index to Losses

In no way does this list attempt to be exhaustive, or mean to suggest that losses exist in singular separateness—surely they often overlap or lead to one another, feeling linked or layered. One stated loss may, of course, indicate other unspoken ones. This list is simply a partial compass, another way to scout among these poems and their vast territories.
—N. S. N.

Index to Poems

Index to Poets